Papunya Tula

ART OF THE WESTERN DESERT

The Papunya Painting Movement,born in the Western Desert in Northern Australia, is now one of the wonders of the modern art world - but its story is not well known.

In 1971, when Geoffrey Bardon, a young Sydney art teacher, was posted to the government settlement at Papunya, he found more than a thousand Aboriginal people living in a state of dislocation and degradation. Bar-don was not the first European to show interest in the traditional sand mosaics of these dispos-sessed people at Papunya, nor the first to recognize them as evidence of a powerful, ancient culture. Anthropologists had studied them ouer many years, but Geoffrey Bardon's empathy with the artists and his parient tribal elders and buought forth reveations in a great surge of creativity hitherto unseen by Europeans.

He provided the painting men with boards, brushes and paints, inviting them to give permanence and portability to a culture which might otherwise have been lost along with the tribal rituals of body decration and images drawn directly in the desert sands.In defiance of the white authorities, he also encour-aged the men to value their work commercially as well as spiritually. By the time he left Papunya in mid-1972, the painting men had formed their own company, Papunya Tula Artists Pty Ltd, with prodigious output, strong sales and great optimism. And the artistic force that had been unleashed continues to this day, albeit with greater self-consciousness and concealment of tribal secrets.

The painting movement set in motion at that time has now spread to other areas of Central Australia and has achieved high inter-national acclaim. Th has not only gone some way to restoring the cultural pride of a deeply religious peo-ple, but it has also provided the rest of the world with a new way of seeing.

This is a book about the exhilaration and the agony of the early days of the Papunya painting movement. It also provides an essen-tial theoretical and tech-nical framework for an adequate 'reading' of the art of the Western Desert. Twenty of thestories of their work. Fifty color reproductions of their paintings are accompanied by diagrams drawn by Judith Ryan, Curator of Aboriginal Art at the National Gallery of Victoria, from sketches and notes made by Geoffrey Bardon and the artists at the time of their miraculous beginnings.

Papunya Tula

ART OF THE WESTERN DESERT

GEOFFREY BARDON

with diagrams by Judith Ryan

JB BOOKS **J.B. BOOKS AUSTRALIA**

This soft cover edition is an exclusive production published in 1999
by J.B. Books Pty Ltd.
PO Box 118, Marlston, South Australia 5033
Phone/Fax (08) 82971669
First publishing in hardback in 1991
by Penguin Books Australia,
487 Maroondah Highway, Ringwood, Victoria 3134.

National Library of Australia
Cataloguing in Publication data
Bardon, Geoffrey, 1940 —
    Papanya Tula: Art of the Western Desert
    Includes index.
    ISBN 0-9586998-6-0
    1. Painting, Australian — Western Desert — Aboriginal artists. 2. Sandpaintings
    2. Title
    759.994

Designed by Noni Edmunds
Typeset in Garamond by Bookset, Melbourne
Printed in Hong Kong
Produced by Phoenix offset

for
Tim Leura Tjapaltjarri
and Johnny Warrangkula Tjupurrula

Old Mick Tjakamarra painting 'Children's Water Dreaming with Possum Story' in 1973 in a transitional hut.

FOREWORD BY JUDITH RYAN

Curator of Aboriginal Art, National Gallery of Victoria

T HE DISPOSSESSED FIRST AUSTRALIANS of the arid Central and Western Desert regions have evolved an exciting contemporary art form, using European materials but based on their own inviolate, mythologically sanctioned designs. It is an art of abstract icon in which an invisible, eternal sense of land and of supernature is rendered visible. It is an art in which *feeling*, *knowing* and *touching* country, kin and spirit world transcend the European imperative to *see*. This unique conceptual art form suffered a difficult birth only nineteen years ago at Papunya – a woebegone government settlement – where free nomadic peoples were brought to 'sit down' and be Europeanized.

The birth and growth of the Papunya Tula art movement owes much to the rare vision of a compassionate young art teacher, Geoffrey Bardon. Angered by the inhumanity and brute racism that confronted Aboriginal people in this 'concentration camp', Bardon won the confidence of a group of older men, and together they set out to prove to white Australians and the rest of the world that Aboriginal art and culture matter and can never be crushed.

In 1971, when Bardon first drove into the wasteland that was the Papunya settlement, he found more than a thousand Anmatjira, Wailpri, Loritja and Pintupi people of great dignity imprisoned under *kardiya* (white) control. The *yapa* (Aboriginal hunter), used to a life of unlimited travel, was reduced to a state of degrading stagnation, cut off from his sources of spiritual power in land. The *karnta* (women), instead of gathering staple foods – seeds, grasses, bush tomatoes, onions, potatoes and plums – were compelled to line up for the processed variety and eat in communal kitchens instead of by campfires. Their spirit still belonged to their country, which had been created by totemic ancestors in the *Jukurrpa* (Dreaming), but the scramble of official buildings, tin shelters, metal and plastic litter, huts, and dirt roads spelt out the ugly incongruity of their current lives.

Bardon saw Aboriginal people in distress, and felt empathy for what they had lost and contempt for the *kardiya* who were trying to trample their unique culture. He noticed, while sitting amongst them in the sand, that they had a form of pictographic writing, or hieroglyphs, that resonated for them with rich stories of their creation from ancestors who were eternally present inside the continent. The self-effacing Bardon was at one with these people, and his imagination was stirred by the symbols that seemed to issue from the land of which they were part. The simple sand doodles, which he was invited to read, struck him as the basis of a new art, the key to another way of seeing the great deserts. The arcs, circles, meanders and tracks he saw were similar to those found on ancient Aboriginal petroglyphs which have been carbon-ratio dated at 31 000 BP, but they were not yet part of the history of Australian art. Bardon made it his mission to rectify this.

Prior to the arrival of this lone art teacher in the wilderness, Western Desert art was confined to ceremony, largely unseen except by the initiated. The only indigenous paintings produced for sale in Central Australia had been those of Aranda watercolorists, working in a transplanted landscape tradition of European making. However, Bardon was not the first white person to take a serious interest in Aboriginal art of the desert regions, or to attempt to decipher the religious significance of the compelling designs. Norman B Tindale, T G H Strehlow, Ronald M Berndt, Charles P Mountford and Nancy D Munn all had preceded Bardon, familiarized themselves with one or more of the desert languages and interpreted the meanings of the largely ephemeral works. Berndt and Mountford, in the course of their own anthropological research, had also given artists sheets of cardboard and crayons, and invited them to transpose the sacred designs traditionally confined to carved boards, body decoration and elaborate three-dimensional ground paintings. Mountford, in 1956, had effectively demonstrated that an Aboriginal youth's drawings alter radically after he has been initiated into the secret-sacred religious world of the men. Instead of sketching part of the landscape as actually seen, the initiate recorded the hitherto-unseen ancestral designs, duplicating sacred objects revealed to him during his own initiation ceremony. None of these anthropologists viewed these designs as 'Art' in their own right, able to be divorced from their ceremonial context. Intent on analysis of iconography, they did not dare to think in terms of Aborigines producing such designs for commercial purposes. Such a focus would have been anathema to them. Bardon, by contrast, as an art teacher, was primarily interested in visual language – the dynamics of color, form and space. This love of art and the inspired impetus to teach were just what was needed to ignite the artists' hitherto-frozen creativity and to nurture its richness.

Bardon's unique achievement was that he inspired authoritative older men to transpose archetypal ritual designs onto board and canvas. The artists were introduced to seemingly incongruous European materials – acrylics, paint brushes, rectangular boards – and were encouraged to speak in their own visual language. Bardon engendered an atmosphere of mutual trust which stirred many elders to begin painting, and this caused a resurgence of cultural pride in the settlement.

The artists were prepared to reveal designs loaded with inner layers of meaning which together constitute a key to Aboriginal mythology, metaphysics and law. Bardon was invited to share this meaning, and to sense the great desert landscape and its secret, named places, from within. The artist in him was excited by the communicative power of the designs. The teacher in him discouraged sloppiness, European-inspired borders and naturalistic imagery, and the use of unmixed pigments.

Such was the artists' enthusiasm and trust in Bardon that, by the time of his departure in mid-1972, about a thousand works had been created. These paintings have the concentrated power of timeless icons and are some of the finest ever produced. Graphic symbols stand out against the dark backdrop, suggestive of the ground or body on which such designs are found in ritual. Each work is singular and adventurous and does not rely on standardized convention. One senses the eternal truths that the artists are revealing by painting not just with their hands but from their whole selves. The small scale results in works with a rare totality of gesture and composition; it is a scale commensurate with the human performer who wears such designs.

In 1972 the artists succeeded in forming their own company with an Aboriginal name: Papunya Tula Artists Pty Ltd. This revolutionary achievement for Aboriginal artists was something Geoffrey Bardon had dreamed of. However, a time of disillusionment followed, as artists were criticized by their peers for having revealed too much of their sacred heritage. Secret designs restricted to a ritual context were now in the marketplace, made visible to *kardiya* outsiders and Aboriginal women. In response to these objections, all detailed depictions of human figures, fully decorated *tjurunga*s (bullroarers) and ceremonial paraphernalia were removed or modified. Such designs and their 'inside' meanings were not to be written down and 'traded'. Any contravention broke the immutable plan of descent, the link of the initiated man with his totemic ancestor through his father and his father's father.

From 1973 to 1975 Papunya Tula artists sought to camouflage overt references to ceremony and became reticent. They revealed less of the sacred heart of their culture. The openness of the Bardon era was at an end. Dotting and over-dotting, as an ideal means of concealing or painting over dangerous, secret designs, became a fashion at this stage. The art was made public, watered down for general exhibition, pointing to the uniqueness of the Bardon years – which, like innocence, cannot be rediscovered.

Also at this time, as if to signal the break with the movement's origins, the historic Papunya school murals were painted over in an unaccountable act of cultural vandalism. The school was de-Aboriginalized and the art no longer allowed to stand tall and defiant as the symbol of a resilient and indomitable people.

In spite of dispiriting setbacks and marketing problems, the Papunya Tula movement strengthened during the 1970s and a pattern was set for expansion to Aboriginal settlements throughout the Central and Western deserts. The movement's success owes much to the sacrifice and foresight of Geoffrey Bardon, whose vital contribution will never be forgotten. After the initial breakthrough, numerous art advisers have followed in Bardon's footsteps, equally anxious to see the painters climb out of their social and economic distress, and passionate in the proselytizing of the art which is still alive and dynamically changing. By the early 1980s many Papunya residents had deserted the dismal township for new communities and outstations closer to their country, such as Kintore and Kiwirr-kurra, where many members of the Pintupi tribe now live. Women have now been encouraged to paint in their own right, instead of being relegated to the apprenticeship role of assisting their male relatives with background dotting.

Each Aboriginal person's totem and conception site or Dreaming is deter-mined by the place in the landscape where the mother experiences her first symptoms of pregnancy. At this place, the unborn fetus is animated by the spirit of a totemic ancestor – water, possum, goanna, old man – with which he will be reunited at death, in the land. The transition from composition board to large canvas that occurred at Papunya in the early 1970s enabled artists to create abstract maps of huge areas of country and to celebrate the journeys of ancestor beings through a succession of named places. The viewer is enclosed in the vastness of the continent conceived as a giant mythscape in which *kuruwarri* (signs or marks of ancestral power) overlap. The desert landscape is depicted not by an alien visitor, perched on the outside, using the brush as a camera, but from inside the very bones of the land. It is not a featureless or empty landscape, but has been humanized and celestialized into a continuous narrative. It is transformed in the Aboriginal imagination into a sacred space in which human, plant, animal and supernatural share the same lifeblood.

One senses in each eternal spring or waterhole the ancestor being awakening from his eternal sleep and bursting up through the earth's crust. The concentric circle condenses this metaphysical concept of the earth being fertilized by living water. It also stands for woman, as child bearer and nurturer, and the camp or home. The interconnecting paths, symbols of the dynamic male travelling principle, follow those of supernatural beings and show where they left their life-giving essence in the land in reservoirs of spirit children. This way of conceptualizing a mighty desert has now taken root in the related Aboriginal desert communities of Balgo Hills, Yuendumu, Mount Allan, Lajamanu and Utopia, among others. And in each of these distinct communities where the Papunya Tula style has been followed, the art has assumed variant style characteristics.

It is hard to believe that the sophisticated canvases now being produced throughout the Central and Western deserts could have sprung from five rudimentary murals painted just nineteen years ago. What nobody could have predicted then is that the seemingly abstract designs painted on anything that came to hand would speak so directly to a white audience accustomed to the visual language of Abstract Expressionism, Conceptualism, Minimalism and Op Art. The rich marriage of ancient indigenous symbols and synthetic European materials has resulted in a powerful new form of modern art which has startled the Australian and international art worlds.

The dotting technique has been appropriated by Aboriginal and white Australian Post Modernists. Papunya Tula art has been exhibited in London, Paris, New York, Mexico City, Madrid, Venice and Montpellier. Large canvases are seen on boardroom walls, in plush hotels and in important collections of Australian contemporary art. Instead of being ignored, the downtrodden and dispossessed first Australians are at last being listened to in their own eloquent language. The acrylic paintings, more potent than any politicized slogans, have enabled the Aboriginal people to assert their fundamental right – the right to land.

The story of the first Papunya years – painful yet exhilarating – is best told by Geoffrey Bardon, because he was there. Bardon saw dignity and strength in the men who had been dispossessed of their land and he fought for their right to speak with their own voice, in art of their making. He recognized dynamism and life in symbols that Strehlow had earlier written off as 'fossilized'. With the artists he suffered the full brunt of white mockery and contempt because he dared to challenge official government policy; he wanted Aboriginal people to escape from white domination and to win. This they have done through their art, as Bardon believed they would. The founding artists are the heroes of this story, inspired by their teacher, Geoffrey Bardon, who chose to stand among them.

FOREWORD BY ULLI BEIER

G EOFFREY BARDON was born in Sydney in 1940. He intended to become a lawyer, but abandoned his law studies after three years because he became interested in art. He then took a course in art education at the National Art School and graduated in 1966. He cannot pinpoint precisely when his interest in Aboriginal culture began, but it was certainly rekindled at art school: 'I learned about theories that say that art grows out of the soil, that it belongs to a particular place, where it was created; that it has a sense of belonging. It's a nationalistic view, put forward by European nations. This made me realize that Aborigines are the ones in this country who have real contact with the land; it is their art that truly belongs to Australia.'

Bardon took several fairly routine teaching jobs in high schools before going to Papunya in 1971. His first contact with Aborigines was at Gunnadah High School, where he had Aboriginal students in his class. They were disorientated, and did not feel that they belonged. Geoff Bardon realized that he did not understand enough about their background to be able to help them. It was this frustration that made him feel he wanted to work with tribal Aborigines. He wanted to be in a situation where he could learn more about their lives and their culture: 'I did not know what I was letting myself into — but that's what I wanted to do.'

He obtained a job at Nightcliff High School in Darwin, but he was not satisfied with that. 'I did not want a fancy job in town, looking for advantages. I wanted to work with Aborigines. So I went to the Welfare Department and told them this.' The Welfare Officer was not encouraging: he told him it would mean a drop in salary and the move would not enhance the development of Bardon's career. He made cryptic comments. What exactly was Bardon up to? What was his motivation for wanting to go and live with Aborigines? But in the end he posted him to a station where no one else wanted to work.

When Geoff Bardon went to Papunya, there were about fourteen hundred people living there, including about seventy-five white people. Some of the Europeans despised Aborigines, and the many who were sympathetic and compassionate didn't seem to make close contact. Bardon, however, fitted in readily.

Geoff Bardon's lifestyle raised eyebrows at Papunya right from the start. People disapproved of this newcomer who often ate his meals in the canteen with the Aborigines, who took them hunting and invited them to his flat. But he was too enthusiastic and too innocent to notice the disapproval. He thrust himself into his work at the school with great energy. Three months after his arrival, he was made the art teacher. He based his teaching on activity programmes. But the children 'were shy to do their own thing'. Outside the class they might play little games in the sand – they would draw spirals and dots and tracks – but in the classroom all they ever wanted to draw were cowboys and horses.

Out of frustration, Geoff Bardon hit on the idea of doing a mural on the school wall. The school was a rather drab building, with cement brick walls, and there was plenty of wall space on the ground floor. Geoff Bardon threw himself into this new project with his usual enthusiasm, but again there were obstacles. 'The kids weren't big enough; they couldn't do it. They got stage fright; they were nervous and confused.'

Then the Aboriginal men who were looking after the schoolyard came forward and offered to paint the mural. They produced a magnificent mural five metres long, then went on to work on a second, more complex wall painting, which included a snake story, a water story, a wallaby story and a widow story.

These two paintings mark the historic beginnings of the Papunya Tula art movement, and it is a sad comment on the cultural awareness of the European community in Papunya that shortly after Geoff Bardon left, both murals were painted out. The murals had caused a small cultural revolution in the camp. The men had discovered that, even away from their ancestral sites in the desert, there could be another dimension to their lives, that there was in fact an intermediate ground, somewhere between the meaningless, bleak existence on a welfare station that was their present, and the intense magic life of the desert that was their past. They were quick to see that Geoff Bardon held the key to this new world, and soon they were trooping up the stairs to the art room of the school where Geoff Bardon was teaching, asking for brushes and boards.

Geoff Bardon spent a lot of time collecting the stories of the paintings and, with the help of Obed Raggett, documenting these diagrammatically.

Geoff Bardon soon realized that the men needed an outlet for their work. He took the paintings to Alice Springs, where he sold them to the Arms Art Gallery. But, while he felt totally in his element working with the painters, he found the business side of things extremely tough. He was not prepared for the difficulties he would encounter. On the one hand the owner of the art gallery pressured him to give her exclusive Australian rights – even world rights – for the paintings, because she understood the commercial potential of these works immediately. On the other hand, the superintendent of the station accused him of 'trafficking in paintings from a government station', and tried to stop him selling the pictures.

In the meantime he continued his work with the men with undiminished commitment. The artists themselves were full of enthusiasm. Geoff Bardon soon found the right language for communicating with them: a bit of pidgin, a few indigenous words. He tried, as soon as possible, to talk to them using their own terms. When criticizing their work he would say things like: 'Too much *munda* (dust)', meaning: there is too much dirt in the water, the colors are not clean.

Bardon was concerned with getting the men to produce traditional designs – to discard all European influences. The men had all seen school books, advertising and movies. At first they tended to introduce borders and realistic elements into their pictures. Geoff Bardon used to tell them: 'Nothing white-fella. No whitefella color, no whitefella perspective, no whitefella images.'

Bardon encouraged the men to work neatly. He was aware of the fact that neatness is not an artistic quality in itself, but he was convinced that for their work to be noticed it had to be 'flash'. He didn't allow everything to go to town to be sold, and through this process of selection he naturally influenced the artists' style: 'Now, for example, I said to Charlie Egalie Tjapaltjarri: "You have not finished that painting. There are not enough dots and they are too big." So he reworked it with small dots.'

The Aboriginal men of Papunya had endured decades of unsympathetic treatment by whites. They were told what to do and what not to do. They had little or no social contact with other white Australians. Geoff Bardon was a different kind of person; he mixed freely with them. He believed in them: 'I believe in God; I believed that I had a duty towards them. The Bible says: "Deny not the innocent what is their due." I could show them what to do and I respected them.'

The Aborigines sensed his enthusiasm and they were inspired by it. 'They were reliable men and very anxious to please, and I was very anxious to please them. And I loved every moment of it.' They knew that he had their interest at heart and that he made no money out of their paintings. So they allowed him to walk around the 'studio', commenting. They responded to his good humour, his warmth and his sincerity.

The movement grew rapidly. Geoff Bardon told everybody that if they wanted to paint they could leave any job they were doing and work for him. He was able to fetch $75–$100 for a Papunya painting in those days, which is not much by today's values but was a lot then, in comparison with what they could earn elsewhere. Geoff Bardon did not endear himself to the Welfare Department through his action, because it lost its gardeners and storekeepers and farm labourers. Geoff was sensitive to the tension he was creating, but as far as he was concerned it was his task to fight for the right of the Aborigine to paint his way: 'completely his way, as he had always done for centuries, and to correctly record it and identify it'.

He observed and recorded the differences in style amongst the various tribal communities:

> The Anmatjira Aranda painted a symmetrical, formalized design. They wanted everything symmetrical and linear. The Loritja and Wailpri were an intermediate group, using flat patterns, with perspective and some symmetry. I use the word *perspective* here advisedly; because whenever you place one object in front of another, you have perspective. It may not be very deep, it may not be a grand vista – but it's perspective. The Pintupi painted flat two-dimensional patterns, and unlike the other groups, they had not been influenced by European art in any way.

Geoff Bardon had the satisfaction of seeing the artists' lives transformed before his eyes. From depressed, unmotivated workers, forced into a lifestyle in which they felt ill at ease, they became enthusiastic and motivated artists. He saw them regain their pride as they began to assert their cultural values. He saw them teaching their children about their traditions through the paintings. He saw them becoming more self-reliant. The money they earned was modest in those days, but it boosted their morale considerably to know that they could be independent of government jobs and welfare work. They were not good at managing their money and they usually spent it quickly. On one occasion, when the men had earned $3000 between them, Geoff Bardon suggested to them that they should invest their money in a truck. 'But they said, "No, we want to buy two trucks. One for the drinkers and one for the non-drinkers."'

Not everybody in Papunya was happy to see the changes. Officials had been used to seeing Aborigines as eternally submissive and dependent. To them Geoff Bardon must have seemed a subversive influence, someone who was rocking the boat. He increasingly became the victim of petty harassment. The pressure mounted unbearably on Geoff Bardon. He was working unbelievably hard in those last months. He was teaching the school children; he was working with the artists; he held evening classes for adults, in which he taught pottery; he edited the school journal. On top of all that, he was making his first documentary film on the Papunya artists. It was as if he felt that time was running out, and he was packing in as much activity as he possibly could. His hectic lifestyle hardly allowed him to eat properly, but he kept driving himself on, 'because I knew that I was doing something important'. To relieve some of the pressure, he applied for a grant from the Australia Council that would allow him to resign from his teaching post and devote his entire time to the artists. He was given a grant of $11 000, but it came too late. A week after he had given up his teaching job, Geoff Bardon became seriously ill and he had to return to Sydney.

He made a slow recovery. He overcame the resistance of the Welfare Department and returned to Papunya to make two more films and to research a book.

In the present Papunya situation, many people have come forward to claim credit for this remarkable artistic movement, including some who opposed it in the early days. The achievement of Geoff Bardon has been pushed more and more into the background. Yet he was a true pioneer; he was the man who had faith in the artists when no one else credited them with any talent whatsoever. He was the one who opened the doors for the Aboriginal community. He broke the taboos of the white community and he paid heavily for it.

Acknowledgements

I wish to acknowledge the advice and support of the Papunya Aboriginal communities, without which this book would not have been possible. I would like to thank Obed Raggett for his tireless help in translation; Ulli Beier for his insights and encouragement; Judith Ryan for her marvellous diagrams and strong support; my parents for their support during the long years; my brother Jim, who read the manuscript and gave it careful consideration; and finally, and most of all, my wife Dorn, who checked every aspect of this work and typed the manuscript.

I would also like to thank Fred Friis for his liberal school policy in 1971, and Allan Scott for his fine photographs of the artists. Other photographers who contributed are Barry Allwright, Jon Falkenmire, Kevin Diflo and Jennifer Isaacs, and George Lindstrom, Grenville Turner and John Williams who photographed the paintings. It has not been possible to locate the paintings on pp. 59, 60, 65, 101, 106 and 116 to have them rephotographed. The transparencies are old and less than perfect.

I wish to thank Dr H C Coombs, Bob Edwards (AO), Margaret Carnegie (OAM) and Dr Joan Grant for their assistance at the beginning of this project, my publishers Hilary McPhee and Diana Gribble, my editor Sally Moss and designer Noni Edmunds. For moral support, Len and Lois Jackson, Jim and Roweena Dunk, Grahame and Bronwyn Norman, and Bert and Ethel Franks.

I wish to thank Val Petering who, in kindness and love towards the Aboriginal people, sold food in the camps to fund Papunya Tula's beginning.

Finally I wish to thank the successive Papunya Tula Artists Company art advisers for continuing this magnificent art movement. They are Peter Fannin, Dick Kimber, Janet Wilson, John Keene, Andrew Crocker and, since 1982, the indefatigable Daphne Williams.

CONTENTS

Old Tom Onion and the author, talking, Papunya, 1971.

PREFACE

THE PAPUNYA SETTLEMENT in the Northern Territory of Australia was established in 1960 and consists of five main tribal groups: Aranda, Anmatjira Aranda, Wailpri, Loritja and Pintupi. Fewer than a thousand people now live in this community and in the surrounding outstations set up since 1972.

Papunya was chosen as the location for settlement because of the availability of bore water; it is not the traditional region for any of the tribal groups. The outstations further west of Papunya are closer to their traditional homelands. But children born at Papunya consider it their home, and through them some 'homeland' stories will still be passed to subsequent generations in accordance with Aboriginal custom.

Most of the artists in the Papunya painting movement are at least forty, are bush trained and have little European education. They speak rudimentary English but respond willingly to encouragement. Until recently they had little awareness of their capacity to resist the social conditioning implicit in the propagation of European values.

The original Papunya painting men are now organized as an independent Aboriginal business known as Papunya Tula Artists Pty Ltd. Such a consensus by men of different backgrounds is a very happy one. Because most of these painters' themes are derived from the traditional myths and stories related to their ancestral territories, which lie west of Papunya, it is accurate to describe their work as Aboriginal art of the Western Desert.

The Dreaming paintings or 'stories' of the Western Desert are about places and occasions a long way from Papunya and are by tribal artists who have inherited an ancient knowledge which will not survive unless it is passed on. (Happily there seems to be among younger people of the community a revival of lapsed interest in this traditional life. However, it is still too soon to say what damage has been done by the distractions of European lifestyles.)

The painting movement at Papunya and beyond has helped to preserve traditional cultural aspirations, protect tribal lands and revive inherited concepts of social order. It continues to be a symbol of hope for greater understanding between two cultures.

INTRODUCTION

The Dreamtime

FOR THE ABORIGINES the Dreamtime is the beginning of knowledge, from which came the laws of existence. It is also the beginning of time, when the supernatural ancestor beings were 'born out of their own eternity'.

The earth was a flat surface, in darkness: a dead, silent world. Unknown forms of life slept below the surface of the land. Then these ancestor beings broke through the crust of the earth from below, with tumultuous force. The sun rose out of the ground. The land received light for the first time. The supernatural beings, or totemic ancestors, were part creature or plant and part human. In all their activities during the creation the ancestor beings behaved as human personalities, with all the attributes and frailties associated with people. They had courage, loyalty, love, friendship, anger and hatred. For example, the possum spirit was an extremely curious personality. The dingo spirit, or wild dog spirit, was good natured and generous but, at the same time, very hostile towards the wallaby spirit. The eagle spirit was very dangerous. The lizard, or goanna, spirit was particularly ferocious.

As the ancestor beings moved across the barren surface of the world, they hunted and fought, and changed the form of the land. In their journeys they created the landscape: the mountains, rivers, trees, waterholes, plains and sandhills. They made all living things: the plants; the birds; the animals; and the people themselves, who are descendants of the Dreamtime ancestors. They made the ant, grasshopper, emu, eagle, crow, parrot, wallaby, kangaroo, lizard, snake and all food plants. They made all the natural elements: water, air, fire. They made all the celestial bodies: the sun, the moon and the stars.

When the creation was completed the stars and all the celestial bodies rose into the sky, and the world of labour, pain and death that men and women have

Mount Leibig gorge. Charlie Tarawa (Tjaruru) Tjungurrayi owned the Pintupi ceremony for this place and painted many versions of the corroboree.

2

known ever since came into being. Then, wearied by all their activity, the mythical creatures sank back into the earth and returned to their state of sleep. Sometimes their spirits turned into rocks or trees or a part of the landscape. These became sacred places to be seen only by initiated men, places where warriors could paint themselves to become invulnerable to spear wounds. They included caves with qualities of special benefit to child-bearing women. These landscape forms and the cycles of nature are evidence of the creation and are the basis of Aboriginal spiritual life.

Corroboree dances reveal the personalities and adventures of the ancestor beings, whose human qualities flow through the Dreaming stories into the totems of the Aboriginal people. All activity of this world – ritual, ceremony, duty – has been decreed by the Dreamtime beings, creating an unchanging, fixed way of life. Knowledge concerning these supreme events is the power and the effective secrecy of Aboriginal society.

All male Aborigines, after full tribal initiation, own a 'Dreaming' (or an explanation of the world and its creation) and are the custodians of its associated stories and songs passed down by their Spirit Ancestors. They in turn have a sacred responsibility to preserve and pass on these stories which revere the life-giving qualities of water, bush tucker and wildlife food, and the importance of fire, medicine and supernatural spirits. Each man can paint or otherwise discuss his personal Dreaming as he inherits it, or as he is permitted by custom. While the specific custody of the subject matter is strictly demarcated by tribal skin groups, each story can be part of a much greater story and might overlap with other stories in the custody of men in other tribes to form a pattern of continuing knowledge and wisdom.

The Dreaming religion is beautiful in thought and in design. With no written word and no records beyond memory itself, the Dreaming world *is* Aboriginal history, spirit-belief, ancestor knowledge, legend, and culture. By its simplification of ideas, it transcends the brutal and the inhuman.

Western Desert Dreaming

In Aboriginal cultures, landscape features (such as mulga, acacia, native grass, gum trees and sandy or stony surfaces) are assigned to family (skin) groups within a tribe and are then further divided between individuals, all of whom

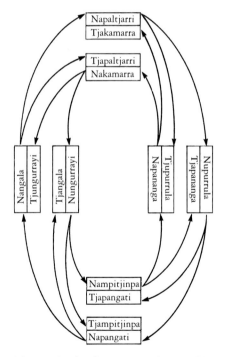

The custody of each painting is determined by tribal skin relationships. There are eight male skin groups (beginning with T) and eight female skin groups (beginning with N). Joined boxes show correct marriage. Arrows point from the marriage partners to the children.

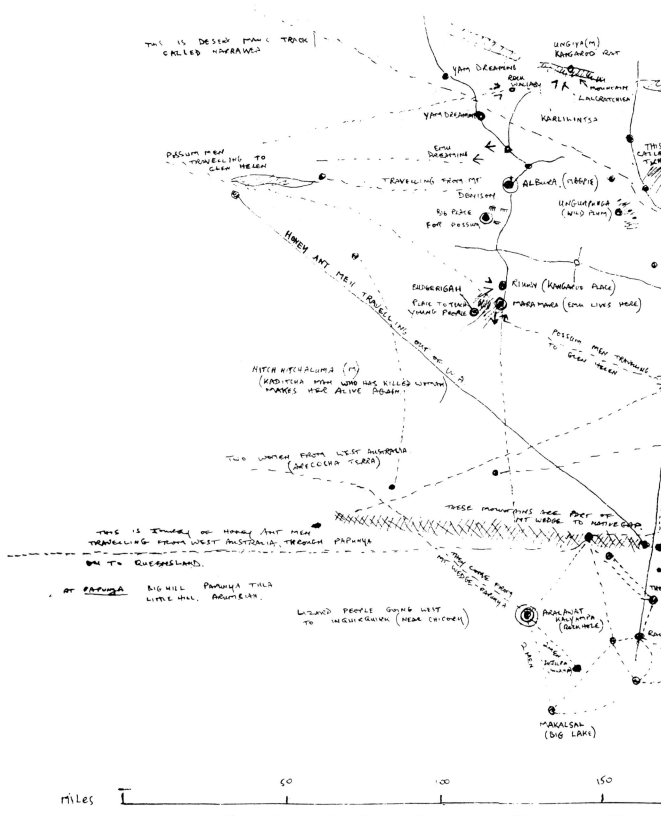

The Dreaming map made by Tim Leura Tjapaltjarri and myself in 1971, showing Tim's ancestral space or Dreaming area around Napperby Station. As it uses neither symbol nor hieroglyph, it is a unique representation.

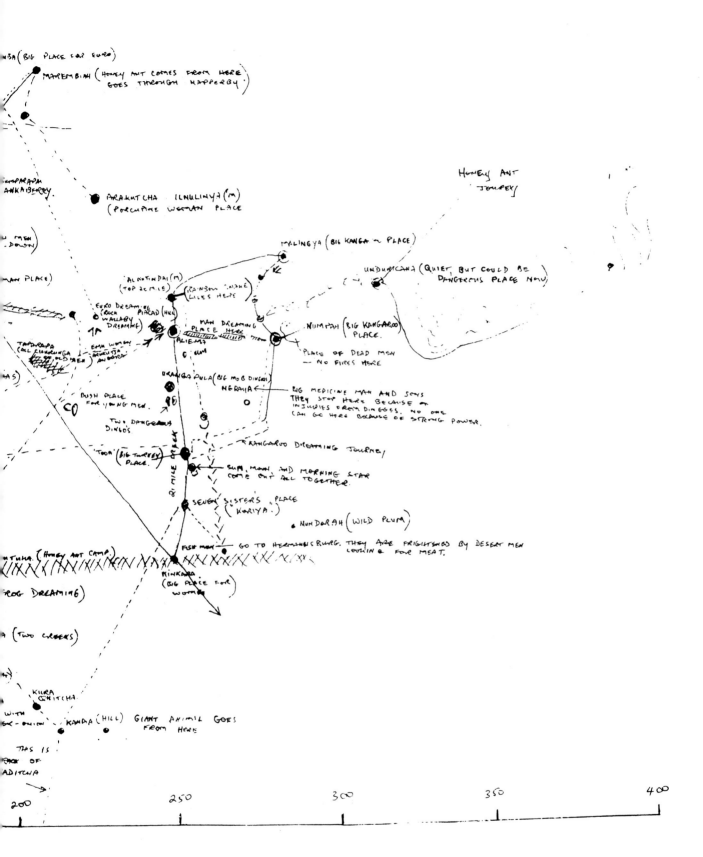

NBA (BIG PLACE FOR EURO)

MAREMBIAH (HONEY ANT COMES FROM HERE)
GOES THROUGH MAPPERBY.)

HONEY ANT
JOURNEY

UUMPARAPA
ANKAIBERRY.

ARAKUTCHA   ILNULINYA (M)
(PORCUPINE WESTERN PLACE

U MEN
DOWN)

MALINGYA (BIG KANGA∼ PLACE)

UNDURICANA (QUIET BUT COULD BE
DANGEROUS PLACE NOW)

MAN PLACE)

ALKOTINDAI (M)
(TOP 2CMIE)

(RAINBOW SNAKE
LIKES HERE

EURO DREAMING
(ROCK
WALLABY
DREAMING)

PIRCAD (HILL)

MAN DREAMING
PLACE HERE

NUMPAH (BIG KANGAROO)
PLACE.

TAPARAPA
(ALL CHURINGA
OLD MEN)

EMU WOMEN
ARAKUTJA
ANDURA

ALIEMA

UM

PLACE OF DEAD MEN
— NO FIRES HERE

HAS)

URANGA PULA (BIG MOB DINGOS)
NERAMA

BIG MEDICINE MAN AND SONS
THEY STOP HERE BECAUSE OF
INJURIES FROM DINGOES. NO ONE
CAN GO HERE BECAUSE OF STRONG POWER.

BUSH PLACE
FOR YOUNG MEN.

TWO DANGEROUS
DINGO'S

'TOOR' (BIG TURKEY)
PLACE.

KANGAROO DREAMING JOURNEY

SUN, MOON AND MORNING STAR
COME OUT ALL TOGETHER.

SEVEN SISTER'S PLACE
('KARIYA.)

MUNDARAH (WILD PLUM)

FISH MEN   GO TO HERMANNSBURG. THEY ARE FRIGHTENED BY DESERT MEN
LOOKING FOR MEAT.

NTUKA. (HONEY ANT CAMP.)

RINKARA
(BIG PLACE FOR
WOMEN

FROG DREAMING)

A (TWO CREEKS)

KURA
CHITCHA.

WITH
X-ONION

KANDA (HILL) GIANT ANIMAL GOES
FROM HERE

THIS IS
BACK OF
ADITCHA

Dried creek bed, Maryvale.

share some part of the Dreaming story of that particular surface feature. Authority over Dreaming myths and ceremonies is in turn divided by the old men and passed on to younger men, women and children in a lifelong process of explanation. All the mysteries of Aboriginal environments and survival are attributed to the ancestor beings of the Dreamtime, so there is an intimate connection between the land surface of any region and the Aboriginal people whose traditional home 'country' it may be. As the landscape changes so do the Dreaming explanations of surface features, natural phenomena such as fire, wind and water, and celestial bodies.

The Western Desert region includes the desert oak, sandhill, and spinifex grass terrain that begins west of Papunya and the tribal regions of the Aranda, the Anmatjira Aranda and the Wailpri. It is the traditional region of the Loritja group whose homeland 'country' is north-north-west of Papunya and borders on the Gibson Desert of Western Australia.

Occupying almost one third of the Australian continent, and most of the State of Western Australia, this stupendous area features flood channels, vast salt lakes, spectacular rock formations and caves, and endless sandhills. It was here, in 1962, that the Pintupi tribe, numbering fewer than five hundred people, were found to have survived the overlapping of Aboriginal cultures in what can only be called a triumph of adaptability.

Contrary to popular belief, it often rains in Central Australia and the Western Desert. Aboriginal mythology concerning the vivid effects of rain and hail in the desert, and the waterholes that survive in dry times, is profoundly lyrical. For more than 30 000 years, Dreaming stories have survived that directly connect with the last Ice Age in Australia, with humans that preceded Aboriginal occupation, and with prehistoric animals and the nomadism required for survival within large traditional areas.

The Macdonnell Ranges are an extraordinary feature of Central Australia. Although of modest elevation, seldom rising above six hundred metres, their prolonged exposure to the weather has produced chasms and landforms that are possibly the oldest yet geologically determined. The ranges cross the lower Northern Territory running east and west for a total of eight hundred kilometres. Rare plants, animals, flowers and insects flourish in the sheltered valleys and rock holes. This is the traditional homeland of the Aranda Aborigines who interpret its surface features as evidence of the Dreamtime creation. The beauty

PHOTOGRAPH: JENNIFER ISAACS

View of the Macdonnell Ranges.

of the ranges is most apparent in the winter months, typically in the early morning and at twilight, when the atmosphere and unique desert light cast violet and blue shadows across the red earth and stone, contrasting with the green plant life along the watercourses.

The traditional Aborigines have poetic empathy with all aspects of this environment. It has become well known through the watercolors of Albert Namatjira and his relatives, mostly Aranda people from Hermannsburg Mission in the western Macdonnell Ranges. However, the Aranda people have been largely detribalized and much of the traditional belief and knowledge of this spectacular Aboriginal culture has been lost or forgotten.

The Anmatjira Aranda group has custody of the flat scrublands that spread north of the ranges. They in turn interpret their own local surface features, rivers, rock formations, hills, trees and subtly changing vegetation, animal, bird and insect life as evidence of the Dreamtime creation of the world. A large group of these people came to Papunya as a result of their involvement with the surrounding cattle stations. However, traditional life remained strong, and distinctive symmetry and subject matter mark the Dreaming designs of these artists.

Territory around Yuendumu and at least 350 kilometres north of the Macdonnell Ranges is the homeland 'country' of the Wailpri group. The terrain

Old Mick Tjakamarra (left) and Old Walter Tjampitjinpa (right). making and touching a ground sand mosaic. The men have on their bodies designs consistent with the meaning of the sand mosaic. The haptic quality of this type of work carried over into the paintings on board.

in this region features occasional rock formations and low hills, river beds, soakages, rock holes, spinifex, sandhills and scrublands. Like those of the Anmatjira Aranda, Wailpri Dreaming myths follow the pattern of ancestor beings entering, travelling and leaving their 'country', thereby creating overlaps with other tribal areas.

Papunya is thirty-three kilometres north of the Macdonnell Ranges and two hundred kilometres west of Alice Springs and is the beginning of desert oak, spinifex and sandhill country. Papunya ground is part not only of the Honey Ant Dreaming but also of the Emu, Kangaroo, Goanna and Soldier Ant Dreamings, all of which involve journeys across the landscape.

It was at the Papunya government settlement in 1971 that tribal men of these different backgrounds and Dreaming environments eventually worked together as one group, crystallizing divergent, contradictory, anonymous, and ancient (yet still shared) beliefs concerning the landscape and the world in which the Aboriginal people lived.

Art and the Dreaming

Aboriginal people learn from childhood to respond to nature, obeying and adoring its forces, and celebrating it in rituals of song, dance and image. Ceremonies unify creatures, plants, stone, life and death, and blend the physical, emotional and spiritual lives of participants. Rather than being separate aesthetic creations, Aboriginal paintings are part of the Dreaming ceremonies. Often they are maps or stories that describe a particular season, animal, place, food or event. More commonly, as among the Pintupi tribe, the paintings are depictions of corroborees which relive the epic journeys made by ancestor beings from very distant places. The painter refers to these places as his 'country' and each painting is a kind of survival map, used to pass on vital information about navigation, natural features, bush tucker and hunting.

The ritual ceremonies and song cycles created by the Dreamtime journeys of the ancestor beings across the landscape are known as 'Tjingari'. These are shared by all of the Western Desert tribal groups, and are the best known of all Dreaming designs. Many of the paintings by the Papunya Tula artists are Tjingari Dreamings, or lesson paintings showing myriad journeys backwards and forwards in a maze of linking and separate paths. Many of the Tjingari ceremonies are strictly 'secret-sacred' and specific details are not to be revealed. To the observer, the works therefore remain unpredictable, brilliant, original yet very private patterns.

The Dreaming stories painted on hardboard or canvas derive in both content and style from Aboriginal sand mosaics, from the body decoration and ornamental headpieces of ceremonial dancers and from various ceremonial objects.

For a sand painting a selected area of ground is prepared by clearing away grass. The surface is made hard by spreading termite-nest gravel, mixed into a paste with water and allowed to set firmly. The area does not necessarily have to be flat. Sometimes various mounds are formed to create a miniature landscape appearance, and the designs of circles, spirals, and loops made from feathers, natural ochres and charcoal are arranged by a special team of men who have custody of the Dreaming story being depicted. Although elaborate and sometimes as large as one hectare, the sand paintings are completely destroyed after the ritual series.

When it is transposed to hardboard or canvas, the ground painting retains its ritual power, and its signs and symbols validly represent the ancient origin, meaning and perception of the landscape.

Most Aboriginal ceremonies, including corroborees, in my experience are restricted to adult male initiates. Neither the ceremonies nor the body decoration, hats and designs used in them may be witnessed by women or children. Such items and designs therefore might not be used in paintings that could be seen by an unrestricted audience. Aboriginal women also have body designs and sacred stones and make some ground designs restricted to them alone.

Body decoration follows a similar process and varies according to the Dreaming subject. In corroboree performances, design elements are used with specific song cycles to invoke the spiritual forces celebrated. Supernatural power pervades the dancers and the sand decorations.

PHOTOGRAPH: GEOFFREY BARDON

Painting by Uta Uta Tjangala, Pintupi, 1971, showing influences of sand mosaic art.

PAPUNYA: 1971

The Settlement

ARRIVED AT PAPUNYA in 1971, very late at night. Millions of insects buzzed about the humble street lights that lit the desert village as I drove my tired VW combi van along the deserted streets. I searched for the superintendent's home and found people there, drunk. In that deep, hot night they showed me my quarters and I was reminded to watch for the view in the morning when daylight arrived. Daylight was very important, as I came to learn, in a place such as this. In that place, it was not only the blind who could not see.

The next morning I looked out of the windows of my flat and saw the stone mountains of the belt-range which ran parallel to the outpost for some sixty kilometres. Later, in the afternoon light, as I recall, there was a shimmering of wild, darkening purple-and-green forms; and then it rained, and a dancing, glistening feeling came from the stone walls of the mountains which were part of the Macdonnell Ranges. They led to Mount Leibig and then further west into the Gibson Desert, from where many of the Aboriginal people had come. I learnt to know these mountains very well after a while, for they would become the intuited superscription of our desert world.

Papunya in 1971 was like a hidden city, unknown on maps because of the shame felt by its Aboriginal inhabitants. The place had a reputation for trouble. There had been riots and serious fighting. I found a community of people in appalling distress, oppressed by a sense of exile from their homelands and committed to remain where they were by direction of the Commonwealth Government. Papunya was filled with twilight people, whether they were black or white, and it was a place of emotional loss and waste, with an air of casual cruelty. I quickly became aware of the breakdown of tribal hierarchies and the disintegration of many of the families.

PHOTOGRAPH: JENNIFER ISAACS

Aboriginal house at Papunya.

I had come to a community of several tribal groups apparently dispossessed of their lands and quite systematically humiliated by the European authorities. It was a brutal place, with a feeling of oppressive and dangerous racism in the air. Although the culture of these people is based on journeys or tracks, and all their Dreamings refer to movement over great distance, the authorities had denied them their birthright to travel. They were frustrated to the point of hopelessness.

There was a continual problem of food supply for the Aborigines, since they had been forced to live off the white people's give-and-take and there was a lack of game for hunting nearby. Sewerage was unsatisfactory and children often put stones down the toilets. Among the children in particular, there was serious disease. Meningitis was endemic and most of the adults were syphilitic. Hepatitis, gastro-enteritis and encephalitis were quite common. Crippled, maimed and disease-ridden children and drunken men and women wandered about aimlessly. There were many deaths while I was there, particularly of small children. You would often hear the mournful wailing and crying of the people from the great camp which surrounded the white settlement.

At night street lights would wander across the centre of the village and come to rest outside the camp toilets. The sky was full of insects, sometimes billions of them, swarming over the lights. There was one very large building: the settlement generator, roaring in the starry desert darkness. Otherwise there was nothing else to see at Papunya at night. The whites closed their doors and went to sleep and the Aboriginal population hugged the night earth in transitional huts, humpies and grass houses.

In daylight the settlement was a rambling sprawl of obsolete buildings, black men and women hurrying to menial work and wild children going off to the school. Narrow dirt roads meandered between army disposal huts. People were purposefully walking in all directions – to the kitchen, the farm, the hospital, the school, and to the hygiene and firewood trucks. The administration office was old, small and like a humpy. So was the hospital, with two European nursing sisters and Aboriginal nursing aids.

There were no trees in the settlement area, except for the school grounds, where young gum trees had recently been planted away from the interference of the younger Aborigines who loved to rest on the school lawns and in the shade at weekends, stripping branches from the trees to use as fly swatters.

Aboriginal cleaning women mopped the government buildings every day. Red dust from the Gibson Desert was a never-ending problem, infiltrating houses, clothes, cars, record players.

In winter the people wore cotton blankets bought from the canteen. Women and children had to go a long way from the settlement to collect firewood. Groups of men, women and children would gather around their own small fires, and the old people would play with the coals in their bare fingers. In the cold months, a smoke haze would hover over the settlement.

During the cyclone wet from the north, the warm rain drops would splash on the soft sand. This was always a soothing, happy time for children. They cried out and laughed and played, just like birds. From the camp all kinds of calls, yells and laughs could be heard, and tiny fires could be seen glowing amongst the glistening corrugated iron and wood of the humpies. Dogs would bark and everything would burst into life. Sometimes torrential rain would flood the people's homes and they would seek shelter on high ground or in settlement sheds. When the road was cut, food would become scarce. The Anmatjira Aranda men loved to go kangaroo hunting. Some, like my friend Tim Leura, were superb with a rifle, particularly in the bush.

The Pintupi camp was the biggest Aboriginal camp and homes were made of bushes and sticks. Some dwellings were made weatherproof by the use of corrugated iron and bags. The Anmatjira Aranda group lived in humpies made from scrap timber and iron. The government plan was to get the people into blockhouses and transitional houses, to be 'improved'. These concrete-and-steel dwellings were considered indestructible and were in neat rows. They were separated by fences of barbed wire. In wet weather they had no drainage.

Not far from Papunya were glades of desert oak, surviving in vast sandhills. There was a wealth of bird life in the desert: budgerigars, pigeons, owls, cockatoos, galahs, eagles, hawks and crows.

Summer was very hot. People still wore clothes as best they could. Many people dressed well and made remarkable efforts to stay clean. Living in grass houses meant that cleanliness was achieved by sweeping with branches and washing in a basin. The people loved their dogs and slept with them at night, especially in winter; yet often the dogs were underfed and diseased. In any season there was a profusion of bush flies.

The school had fourteen teachers and was quite modern. The difficulty of inducing the Aboriginal children – especially the Pintupi – just to attend school represented cultural incompatibility. The European expectation of regular attendance was quite contrary to all Aboriginal teaching traditions, whereby young people, until adolescence, are allowed complete freedom in preparation for the hard responsibilities of later life. (Eventually I moved out of the European school and taught the Pintupi children in the Pintupi camp itself. A large hut was built for this purpose.)

Most of the teachers worked hard to advance the children, and progress was being made. Some teachers did not care if the children did not attend, and others drove out to the camps to get them. The children seemed to learn by repetition and loved pencils, paper, soap and combs. They were not allowed to speak their

Two Pintupi girls at Papunya.

own languages at school and Aboriginal drawing was of cowboys and horses, never indigenous design. Because of my lesson methods the children came to call me 'Mr Patterns'. When they were not at school, the girls often played softball and the boys played football. Sometimes they were allowed to do this all day, several days running. This freedom was known as the 'jollies'.

One of the highest priorities in the settlement was to get a car ride – anywhere, any time. The children would never tire of asking for a ride. In summer the most popular destinations were the Five Mile bore, the dam or the Mount Lawrie waterholes, where they could have a swim. They loved to show off and please the white people taking them. They were conditioned to please and genuinely wanted to.

There was chronic idleness on the settlement. Of more than four hundred men, fewer than ninety worked and about twenty-five were managed or assisted by me. Work roll-call was at 7 a.m. The outpost manager who called the roll was part Aboriginal, as were most of the go-betweens of the blacks and whites. Some of the Anmatjira Arandas said they were treated like cattle. The black people were being trained in 'proper work habits'. Capacities varied widely. Clifford Possum and Bill Stockman, who were Anmatjira Aranda, could repair cars, guns and so on, but few Pintupi men could drive or hunt with a gun. Yet their marvellous eyesight enabled them to read tracks in the sand. The Pintupi men were employed sawing wood for the white stoves. This was part of their 'training' allowance. Other men hosed lawns all day. A special group gathered firewood with a tractor.

The Aboriginal people at Papunya could be considered uncomfortable, unhappy and in distress. They were faced with humiliation and degradation and the management of the outpost provoked conflict and turmoil.

One Saturday night in May 1972, the extraordinarily passive Aboriginal folk rioted. The settlement pistol was stolen and the police fired at night over the heads of the rioting children. Thirty police arrived the next day. Ten children were sentenced to a total of seventy-four years' gaol as a result of the riot. (Gaol for them was a place with three meals a day and pictures on Sunday.) The superintendent's pistol was never recovered, and the episode was blamed on petrol sniffing and alcohol, not on the frustration of a brutal captivity.

There was a disturbing changeover of staff at the Papunya settlement and the Aboriginal people seldom made contacts of any substance. Doctors and sisters were always hurrying impatiently. Aborigines were not allowed near white homes. One man threatened to shoot when Aboriginal children approached. This same man kept urine in his empty flagons just in case his flat was burgled by blacks. He live there for ten years. One assistant superintendent made booming tarzan yells over the Aboriginal camps. The mechanic said he would not help Aborigines with their cars because 'if you helped one you would have to help them all'. The carpenter took six months' leave without a replacement. The police sergeant's wife had not spoken to an Aborigine in years. There was very little social work done to help the Aboriginal families.

Many whites felt great hatred towards the Aborigines. Whites refused to shake hands with them for fear of catching diseases. Blacks were seldom allowed in government cars or any white car at all. All about the settlement were filth and dissolution. If the Aborigines left a water tap dripping, the settlement superintendent would switch off the water to that part of the camp as punishment. There was a great deal of white theft of Aboriginal food and beer from the kitchen. Anything could be taken from Aborigines without effective protest.

One night I was disturbed by a knock on the door of my flat. It was Nosepeg Tjupurrula and his wife, with their sick baby. The Aborigines were not allowed to come to the white quarters but he was looking for the nursing sister. He described her not in words but by gesture. She had a huge body and a square head and was two metres tall. He was frightened to go to her door. Aborigines know when you don't like them. The baby died.

The white community at Papunya was divided into two groups: the drinkers and the churchies. Each group bitterly disapproved of the other. The drinkers mostly loathed Aborigines and their sessions often ended in fist fights. They would travel vast distances for these occasions. The churchies were far more compassionate towards the black people.

On Sundays Lutheran services were held by the Pastor in the morning and evening. Around the small mission church were many beautiful flowering bougainvilleas. There was a mixed congregation of white and black, with many Aboriginal children who wandered about during the service. The lessons were read in Aranda and the Pastor's daughter played the organ. Long Jack Phillipus Tjakamarra and Johnny Warrangkula Tjupurrula, both painting men, were devout Christians. The whole community thought Pastor Petering a good bloke. The people loved to sing the hymns and the strong nasal harmony was very stirring, a kind of strange and muted affirmation of themselves.

The policemen at Papunya lived with their families in a separate compound away from the settlement. There was a new court house and a gaol, called the 'monkey house'. Because the Aboriginal people were in gaol often, they felt that they knew the police well. The police had a black tracker and savage guard dogs. They fed kangaroo meat to the dogs and this upset the Aborigines very much.

The sacred tree for the Honey Ant Dreaming journey was in the police compound and was shielded by a very high fence. I often thought that the irony of this was quite lost on the Europeans at the settlement, the majority of whom acted like cultural sleep walkers.

Once a week pictures were screened at Papunya. Cowboy and horse films were most popular. When sea and love films were shown, the screen would be pelted with stones and rubbish, leading to cancellation of all films for a time.

The canteen was the only place the people could get food, and this was possible only if they had money. The canteen was often broken into. Reprisals would take the form of a hunt down of the offenders and closure of the canteen to the black community for a day or two. Because the offenders were usually children the superintendent blamed the school programme. Quite often the canteen ran out of supplies upon which the people depended: flour, bread, sugar, tea; yet there was no reason for this to happen, except during floods.

The roaring generator and the big canteen were a constant reminder of the captivity of the people on this settlement, in particular the Pintupi group from the Gibson Desert of sandhills and spinifex. These people had known whites for only ten years and felt particularly trapped in their areas around the settlement. Ultimately this domestication of the Pintupi brought misunderstanding, disease and death in this pestilential cesspool. Yet the people were not allowed to leave.

Outside Papunya, outpost tracks led in all directions. White people would say the blacks were different, and very happy in the bush, travelling and resting at places where they could not hear the generator.

Working with the Children

The children I was to teach were divided into pre-school, primary and high school groups. I taught in English, but found that most of the children had only a limited command of the language. My assistant, Obed Raggett, was invaluable. He would reiterate in Pintupi what I was asking of the children and his being there brought forth a better response. Later I acquired a working knowledge of Pintupi, but Obed Raggett continued to be a marvellous intermediary, and a very great deal of my achievement is owed to his openness as a person and his love for the designs that emerged through our work.

In the mornings the children would close in on the school in silence, their clothes a yellowish grey, their skin dusty and hair matted. They were required to have a shower with soap every day before classes began. Only then could they have fruit at morning tea and a hot lunch for ten cents. After school they would change back into their camp clothes and return to the filth they were taught to despise, into the custody of Aboriginal adults who had no real control over their own lives.

When I began working as an art teacher at Papunya I would observe the children, both tiny and not so tiny, playing games and making finger designs in the sand. They had none of the overwhelming sense of despair and self-hate, loss and dereliction so apparent in the adults, but instead were brimming over with exuberance and innocence. I would stand among the spinifex with the red sand dunes about, surrounded by sinuous lines that were images of water or possum or kangaroo. The children would be whispering and laughing softly, or singing together and sometimes clapping their hands, while smoothing out the sand and lovingly making circular and tjurunga shapes with their fingers.

And so it was, within a few days of my arrival at Papunya, that I saw in the humble red sand beneath my feet the children's outlines of the Aboriginal designs, and in them the ultimate meaning of the centre of our continent. This vivid sight was what led me to seek out explanations for the designs being used and thus to form the beginnings of the Western Desert painting movement.

My initial wish, to foster indigenous design through the school classrooms, met with little interest from the children. I assumed that this was due to ignorance of their own tribal culture, which turned out to be only partly correct. The truth was that they felt that tribal design would not be liked or understood. A single act of self-assertion could not undo generations of neglect and the damning lack of self-esteem in the Aboriginal community.

At first the children were very shy and uncertain about how to respond when I encouraged them to do line drawings for silk screens or simply as exercises. I would ask for a line drawing of a kangaroo or grub and they would give me an outline. I would then show it to the other children in the class and ask them to do the same. Eventually I encouraged them to fill in these outlines, using their

Kangaroo by Amos

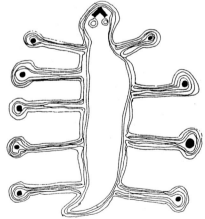

Grub by Nita

Designs made by the children at Papunya School in 1971.

17

own patterns and markings, and this was how I acquired the affectionate nickname 'Mr Patterns'.

Bill Stockman later told me, after a number of lessons such as these, that a meeting of Aboriginal men had been held and it had been decided to allow the children to make their drawing designs available to me, and to help me. From then on, when I asked the children what a design meant, they freely told me.

The drawings were attached to the classroom walls so that the children could understand that the white man's classroom was now letting them see what their culture had produced using the white man's artefacts. There was a gentle supportiveness in this, though: an invitation to them to understand that they were equal to the whites. It was important that they not feel any obligation to me as a white person. I did not want a hierarchy of skin colors, but only a kind of mutuality and love. I did not interfere with their drawings other than to say over and over that what they did should be clear and direct and true.

Perhaps in those days I was seeking truthfulness itself, for the truthfulness would always come and there suddenly seemed no end to what the children would draw. They had found it quite natural to be themselves, even in the white man's teaching room.

In July 1971 I suggested to Fred Friis, the school headmaster, that a school magazine be brought out. He readily agreed, so I brought out four editions of the school magazine in what remained of that year. I was the editor and general writer for all four editions.

I reproduced in each edition of the magazine two or more line drawings by the children in my care. I felt that, if the children saw their own work – their cultural self-perception – in print, they would view their heritage in a wider context.

And so they did: the children became more and more responsive. It gave me great joy to have them show me, a European, the way they understood the world about them.

The School Murals

Over a period of time my efforts in directing the children towards traditional Aboriginal patterns led to a school project for painting decorative murals

PHOTOGRAPH: ALLAN SCOTT

The first mural painted at my request, in 1971, on the school wall. It was painted over by the authorities after I left Papunya in 1972. The mural represents the Honey Ant Dreaming story at Papunya, the main mythology of Central Australia.

on several shabby, unpainted walls below the classrooms, which were mounted on steel columns.

Although the young Aboriginal people, some as old as fifteen and sixteen, could not or would not do this work very well, the school gardeners and maintenance workers, the local handymen and the old men pensioners freely offered to contribute. They began with a very simple Aboriginal pattern of zig-zags and spirals on a small neglected wall. The result was very attractive. The regular school yardmen, Bill Stockman Tjapaltjarri and Long Jack Phillipus Tjakamarra, wanted to help. Money raised by selling food in the Aboriginal camps every pay fortnight funded the complete repainting of all the blank walls under the school classrooms and the steel columns themselves.

During this time (May to August 1971) I met the various Aboriginal leaders who were in fact the most important old men: Old Mick Tjakamarra, Old Walter Tjampitjinpa, Old Bert Tjakamarra, Old Tutuma Tjapangati and Old Tom Onion Tjapangati. These men showed great curiosity about what the school projects were achieving and probably were interested in finding out what kind of man I was.

I began to understand that the murals had to satisfy an Aboriginal community that was split quite dramatically into tribal groups and families, and people of widely different backgrounds, experience and beliefs. In particular they had to be such that they could be seen by women and young people. If the subject matter were not acceptable to all these diverse groups, disputes and hostility could arise within the Papunya Aboriginal community just as they had at other settlements, missions and cattle stations.

As a climax to the mural painting, a special feature wall in the area underneath the school classrooms was carefully prepared with a cement-rendered surface. Any mural painted on this ten-by-three-metre wall would dominate the entire school lawns and playing area. It was a major undertaking and the design became a subject for serious negotiations with the old men.

Kaapa Tjampitjinpa became known to me as the principal artist in the undertaking. No money was to be paid for any of the painting. In retrospect I realized that the Papunya men liked the small murals and columns and now were seriously going to 'give' a design of some importance in response to the general goodwill, enthusiasm and acceptance of the other wall decorations. By this time I had been at the settlement six months and had become known to the leading personalities, four village councillors, teaching assistants, and the school yardmen.

I recall most vividly a group of Aboriginal men, some of whom I had not met before, knocking at the door of my flat one cold night, and silently filing in. They sat in their clothes all crushed and seemingly used up and it was then that I first saw Kaapa Tjampitjinpa, as himself. He secretively handed a piece of paper to Old Mick Tjakamarra and kept whispering and making signs to Mick to hand the paper to me. There were gestures and coughing and the clearing of throats, and at last the paper was handed to me. I unfolded it and this fellow, as yet unnamed and unintroduced, pointed at it from where he stood and said, 'Design'. I nodded, and looked at it. It was a rough composite drawing of the mural they planned to paint on the school wall – a series of lines and what seemed like arabesques, but all very simple and basic. I realized there would be a problem filling such a large area and supplying materials for the task. This outline was the first conceptualization of the great honey ant mural, the first public affirmation of Aboriginal culture at Papunya.

A few days later seven men, including Long Jack and Bill Stockman, began to paint on the so-far-empty wall. I noticed that the alert fellow, whom I now knew as Kaapa, seemed to be in charge of the other painters, telling them what to do. Then, because of what seemed to be a strangely tenuous approach to the mural details, I decided to intervene in what was being done. I pointed at the wall and said to this Kaapa, who seemed to know everything and everybody, 'Are these ants proper Aboriginal honey ants? Nothing is to be white fellow.' All the work suddenly stopped and six other painters crowded about to look at the honey ants. Kaapa seemed to have the answer even before the words were said. He liked to push himself towards you with a distinct movement of his face, a roughish, all-knowing look, all quick and right. 'Not ours,' he said. 'Yours.' 'Well paint yours,' I said, '– Aboriginal honey ants.' He looked at me for a second and went across to Bill Stockman and Long Jack. After a few whispered words he came back and took up his brush and made the honey ant figure, or hieroglyph, then made true travelling marks around the true honey ant.

It was quite a moment, as we all watched – Old Bert, Old Mick, Bill Stockman and Long Jack and the others – the first hieroglyph being put on the wall lovingly and beautifully, with a marvellous painting technique. Some of the men went across and touched the wall even before the paint had dried. Then the little children came across and stood beside the old painting men and Kaapa, and we all stood back and watched the start of the honey ant mural as it was finally to appear. This was the beginning of the Western Desert painting movement, when, led by Kaapa, the Aboriginal men saw themselves in their own image before their very eyes, on a European building. Something strange and marvellous was set in motion.

The steel poles supporting the building were painted white, with a smart yellow band at the tops and bottoms. They were now an elegant colonnade complementing the white walls covered with striking murals. Much of the wall painting was done by the school classes, by Obed Raggett and by me. Some of the columns were decorated by Kaapa, Bill Stockman and Long Jack, who had been allowed substantial time off their daily schoolyard duties for this specific purpose.

THE PAINTING MOVEMENT: 1971–72

The Early Days

AS AN ART TEACHER and an artist myself I had considerable interest in Aboriginal graphic design. Also, I wanted to see how these artists had learned what they knew. For this reason I later continued my involvement with the painters long beyond a point most Europeans would have considered appropriate. I felt this sustained contact was necessary to achieve a response from the men. Though I did not realize it at the time, my willingness to share their perceptions prepared the way for the wide community acceptance and support I was to be given. I was treated as a friend, a contact, a customer. Perhaps most importantly, I was a supplier of painting materials.

Two regular members of my shooting team were Johnny Warrangkula and Mick Namerari Tjapaltjarri who, with others, were very interested in the paints I had in my classroom and living quarters. To get to know the men, I often drove them to their camps after shooting. I took advantage of any chance to see their world more closely.

At this time, Kaapa Tjampitjinpa also painted occasionally, working with various men in the abandoned old settlement office. This was a distinctively squat, unimposing building with a plaque on the wall outside stating that the settlement had been opened by the Minister for Territories, Mr Paul Hasluck. On the floor of the enclosed verandah and interior room, old tins and various receptacles were scattered. Leaning against the walls were pieces of cardboard, fibre, school slates and scrap masonite. It was here that I got to know the older painters, particularly Old Mick and Old Walter. It took a long time to know these men. They were in no way friendly and my impression was that they wondered why I was interested in them. Yet, in spite of their apparent reservations, they were courteous. Whilst they were very industrious in acquiring their own boards to paint on (any flat surface would do, of any material, shape or thickness), brushes and paint were the problem, and I was seen as a good bloke because I had materials in my schoolroom.

Later, Tom Onion explained that it was he who had 'given' me the Honey Ant Dreaming at the school and that if I forgot it and didn't reward him for his authority over this long period of time he would be 'crash angry'. (He said this quickly, glaring at me with his good eye and showing the white of his blind eye.) I acknowledged the importance of his help in having the honey ant mural painted on the school wall at the very beginning of my contact with the men, and promised to help him. He was quietened, apologized and laughed in a knowing way. He had helped me and now it was my turn to help him. This was a fair custom, but one which was sometimes disregarded by the whites.

Johnny Warrangkula Tjupurrula, Mick Namerari Tjapaltjarri, Paddy Tjangala and Kingsley Tjungurrayi were village councillors with a great deal of spare time and an urge to paint. The police tracker, Limpy Tjapanganga, also showed great interest. These old men centred their enthusiasm around the energy shown by Kaapa.

Kaapa, I always felt, had been badly intimidated by the whites, in spite of his courage and determination. When I saw his work in the early days he seemed very often to use European forms for animals, insects and birds in his paintings. I used to insist (as best I could, because he was a very proud man) that he should use Aboriginal forms, but he did so only hesitantly. He was not strictly a tribal Aborigine because he had worked as a stockman. He was an Anmatjira Aranda and I had the feeling that these people, mid-way between the Europeans and the tribally affiliated Pintupi, had been subtly compromised in their culture by connection with the whites. Kaapa had to be told to come back to his true self and see himself wholly, and I am sure he eventually did. Perhaps all he needed was a complaint spoken a few times in his ear. He was a magnificent and naturally gifted painter, a technician of immense ability. And he purified his paintings as he went. (I even recall how in a moment of great joy I gave Kaapa a compass to show him how to draw circles. But Kaapa drew better circles than any compass anyone ever made, as I found out – and, moreover, with his eyes closed.)

At first Kaapa did not like to paint with children around, but later he joined Bill Stockman and Long Jack who worked regularly at the back of the schoolroom. They painted in a kind of barricade of tables, chairs and masonite panels which created the illusion that they weren't behind the little children, though of course they were.

I could always tell when I had a visitor in that anonymous back section of the classroom for I could make out the steady, full steps of the painters coming up the stairs and then a great silence as they sat down to work. This was where the painting movement began, before later moving to the 'painting room'.

The men showed no concern for the technical quality of each other's work and seldom discussed what they were individually painting. Materially, too, each man had his own requirements. As a stop-gap measure I supplied old brushes, old paint and the masonite ends of fruit crates that the school rations arrived in. Sawn-up old tables were also used as painting boards. The school provided money to buy timber off-cuts and quality board from the Alice Springs timber yard. These were consumed at a tremendous pace. More money raised from selling food on pay fortnights bought further board, paint and brushes. I had a sense of exhilaration in the wild zeal which the men now applied to the work. For all of the men, painting seemed to be a primary form of self-expression, so it was hard for me (practically and in conscience) to show any preferences.

The majority of the population at Papunya was made up of the gentle but unconfiding Pintupi people. They seemed to me often to have little idea of the importance of secret-sacred paintings. Uta Uta Tjangala in particular often used to paint corroboree hats for exhibition at the school and Tim Leura and other Anmatjira Aranda took exception to this. I sensed an almost total lack of understanding and control between the Pintupi and those Aboriginal groups who had long contact with the Europeans.

The Pintupi knew almost no English and seemed to have no wish to learn it. They were the quintessential desert nomads and I was often saddened by their sense of loss and dispossession at Papunya. They were magnificent-looking people and they could certainly lift their spirits; but, among the older people in particular, there was an air of melancholy which seemed only to change when they began to paint.

Tim Payungka was a traditional Pintupi hunter and he had an exquisite eight-year-old daughter named Laura, who was in my class at the Pintupi camp. After the roll-call of workers early in the morning outside the settlement office Tim Payungka and a number of other Pintupi had to walk past my flat to get to the settlement farm, and they would sometimes call in.

Aborigines were not officially allowed into the white living areas as there had been occasions of burglary and nuisance. It was not common to do as I did, allowing men into my flat and giving them cups of tea and food, sometimes fifteen at a time. The flat was spacious, with a kitchenette and wooden ceiling, was air conditioned and had a very private carport where my visitors could sit down and talk. Uta Uta and another Pintupi painter, Yaata, were regular visitors and asked for biscuits and cups of tea. I would give the men pieces of paper on which to make designs. When I asked what each design meant, Tim and the others very readily told me. If treated sincerely as equals the Pintupi showed themselves to be full of life and always wishing to explain what a drawing was and what place it depicted.

Because of their limited contact with European ways the Pintupi's painting method was only slightly removed from decorating sand with grass, feathers and ochre. Their designs were simple, stylized shapes or a linear maze, with elementary ornamentation, showing a raw and sensual technique.

They were skilful at drawing and would use the reverse end of a brush or a twig for dotting. These men had a pleasing candour and lack of sophistication, and their painting had the immediacy of a culture that still depended on bush life. A certain derision was shown by the other painting men towards the Pintupi because they were so simple. Pintupi children suffered similar ridicule and many would not attend the school because of this.

Contact with Pintupi men on the settlement soon made me widely known to the entire community, despite the forbidding nature of this rejected group. When Yaata and Uta Uta began coming to my flat, other Pintupi men who worked chopping wood at the settlement farm began to come also, wanting to draw and paint. My teaching assignments over the years had enabled me to accumulate a very substantial quantity of waste art materials – crayons, pencils and inks. They would pick up any of these materials from the verandah and use them to create an unending series of 'Dreamings' and 'my country'. Most of these were concentric circles with curved loops, linked by spiralling lines in an overall pattern. There were many variations. Occasionally there was a nervous scribble, like an attempt to write. With tremendous intensity and speed they recorded their Dreamings, drawing on both sides of the paper or on top of work that was already finished, quite unconcerned at spoiling the first drawing. There were clear differences in many of the pencil designs. Some were exquisitely sensitive.

Pintupi Dreaming designs (pencil on paper) done outside my flat in 1971.

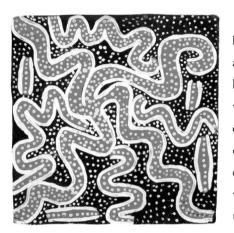

'*Snake Dreaming*' *by Charlie Tarawa (Tjaruru) Tjungurrayi (Pintupi). 1971, poster paint and PVA on a thirty-centimetre-square floor tile. Small paintings such as this were completed on linoleum tiles in the very early days of the painting movement. The painting shows great vigour and resourcefulness in telling a story in a confined area. There was never any use of space for its own sake. The use of large areas of canvas or board to tell trite or common-place stories has been a recent development, reflecting upon the superficialities of European culture.*

At this time workmen were putting new lino tiles into many of the European houses at Papunya. Old tiles were stacked outside the homes to be taken away and dumped. They were thirty centimetres square. The Pintupi men began bringing these to the flat and asking for paint. They had almost certainly heard what the other men were doing in the school art room and the old settlement office. They asked for boards, then brushes, and then paints. They came every day for some time and, when not busy at the wood yard, would settle down outside my flat working. Then they would come early in the morning on their way between roll-call and the wood yard. Their polite laughing and shuffling on the verandah would wake me. These visits were to arrange for boards, brushes and paint to work at lunchtime. If I made myself available to talk, each man would quickly make his own special request in rudimentary English. It seemed fair that if other men in the art room had boards provided, then so should the Pintupi from the wood yard.

I began to know these humble men quite well during the months from September to December 1971. They constantly showed me their work, occasionally calling for 'pencil' and 'more paper'. Soon they were waiting for me at the flat every lunch hour. They did not want to chop wood any longer. The settlement manager had refused to pay them their 'training allowance' if they did not do their work at the wood yard. It became necessary for me to restrain them from coming to my flat, for their own good. However, they continued to come.

They now bought their own scrap wood and fibro. This was sometimes shaped into elongated ovals similar to tjurungas, and they would decorate it with ink and scrap tubes of school paint. The colors were often blue, green and purple but the striking and clever designs were uniquely Aboriginal. Only when the men's work was admired, and an atmosphere of acceptance established, would the children in my classes paint simple stories in the same manner.

The 'painting men', as they became known, were scattered all about the place, working in small groups. There were Kaapa and Bill Stockman and Long Jack in their barricaded space behind the classroom. There were others, such as Old Walter Tjampitjinpa, Old Tutuma and Charlie Tarawa (Tjaruru), working under the school. In the old settlement office there were Old Mick Tjakamarra, Old Don (who was murdered in Alice Springs while I was at Papunya), Nosepeg Tjupurrula, Johnny Scobie, Johnny Warrangkula and Mick Namerari. There were also many casual painters at my flat: Tim Payungka, Anatjari No. I and Anatjari No. III, Freddy West Tjakamarra, John Tjapaltjarri, Shorty Lungkata,

PHOTOGRAPH: FRED FRIIS

Most of the painting men, with the author, outside the Papunya painting room at the east end of the 'Town Hall' hut, 1971.

Uta, Yaata, Tommy Tjampitjinpa and other casual Pintupi painters from the farm. All this painting would be going on during the day while I was working, and the numbers of men painting at any one time would fluctuate.

The painting activity seemed to bring the men together in a way which hadn't occurred before except on ceremonial and unique occasions. It seemed to release them back into their own culture.

When the old settlement office was closed to make way for European living quarters, the painters were all brought into the art room. However, the men were not happy with the presence of Aboriginal women and children, some of whom came to the twice-weekly evening art classes I ran. The painters were therefore allowed to work in a storage room at the eastern end of a building which had been the Town Hall. The timber and building supplies were removed from this part of the building and the painters divided their time between the art room and this new painting room. Uta Uta and Yaata, with Tommy Tjampitjinpa, would divide their time between my flat and the school art room, where the basic materials were readily available. The Pintupi group from the wood yard and farm continued to work outside my flat.

The absenteeism of Aboriginal men from maintenance jobs in gardening and hygiene, at the wood yard and the farm, in the schoolyard and on the village council had caused consternation among the settlement administration. With the advent of commercial success and Mr Friis acting as an intermediary, permission was given for the men to continue painting 'for me', with concession for time off, and still receive their 'training allowance'.

The Painting Group

The Papunya Tula artists had a variety of daytime occupations. While I was at the settlement Johnny Warrangkula Tjupurrula and Mick Namerari Tjapaltjarri were village councillors; Bill Stockman Tjapaltjarri and Long Jack Phillipus Tjakamarra were school yardmen; Uta Uta Tjangala was a gardener; Anatjari No. III Tjakamarra was a maintenance worker; and Tim Payungka Tjapangati, Yala Yala Gibbs Tjungurrayi, John Tjakamarra and Freddy West Tjakamarra were Pintupi farm workers.

They were men from different tribes and different homelands, custodians of myriad Dreaming topics that were connected by a shared landscape, who came together to work as one painting group. They worked in harmony despite their differences of background and despite the threat that policies then in force would terminate Aboriginal art and culture during their lifetimes. Few European educators had any knowledge of the full range and nature of these people's art, even though it had been the principal ceremonial decoration of the Central Australian tribes long before European contact.

The most independent men in the community, possibly those who had the most contacts with European lifestyles, were the very last to join the group. These men were Kaapa Tjampitjinpa, Clifford Possum Tjapaltjarri and Johnny Lynch Tjapangati, all of whom had been stockmen and belonged to the Anmatjira Aranda group. Other latecomers were David Corby Tjapaltjarri and Charlie Egalie Tjapaltjarri, both Wailpri men, who were brothers and had similar cattle station backgrounds in districts north of Papunya. Shorty Lung-kata Tjungurrayi was also one of the last men to join. He had some special eminence in the Pintupi group and made himself known long after the Pintupi men had begun full-time painting.

Old Walter, Old Mick and Old Tutuma had often sat in the sun under the school art room when the murals were being painted. Old Walter was something of a gentle and kind patron in my gradually improving understanding of the

PHOTOGRAPH: ALLAN SCOTT

Left to right: John Tjakamarra, Freddy West Tjapaltjarri, Anatjari No. III Tjakamarra, Charlie Tjakamarra (singing) and Tim Payungka Tjapangati – all Pintupi men – at Papunya in 1971. The men had been told there would be a 'photo time', when all the 'painting mob' would have their photograph taken. I asked for good flash shaving and best clothes 'to catch the people in Australia'.

Aboriginal way of life. Later he told me that he was the custodian of the Water Dreaming and his many variations on this theme afforded me knowledge of ceremonial sites and special places, such as Kalipimpinpa, which were part of the journeys in what seemed to be an uncharted wilderness west of Papunya into the Gibson Desert.

The painters would begin work in the painting room at about 8 o'clock each morning. They would come in twos and threes and set up their boards, or simply sit down before a painting which had been begun some days or weeks ago. Each painter had a certain place within the former Army cupola hut, which had since been both a storage area and a town hall. The room had four electric lights with dish shades hanging from a steel-framed, arched roof. Aged, rusty meshing partitioned the painting room from the murky, cavernous 'Town Hall'. This other section contained a trampoline, a piano and several tables where the Lutheran Pastor conducted the weekly 'bank' for the native people. The painting men had carefully covered any openings in this partition, and the painting room

Long Jack Phillipus Tjakamarra (left) and Johnny Warrangkula Tjupurrula (right) working in the painting room in June 1972.

was like a big cave. Although the louvred windows were always closed (and covered with mesh) dust would constantly find its way into the room. There was a tap in the room providing water from the main water tower, but no drain. The bucket that was used was always filthy and overflowing across one low part of the floor. It never occurred to the men to empty it, and sometimes paintings would become water damaged.

Scattered across the floor were various tins, tubes, lids and boards. I remember very clearly the strange inward-flowing light of the huge room whose door was always shut. It was important, so I found, for the men to have a sense of belonging, and a certain rightness of place when twenty to thirty of them were in the painting room, whistling, singing and chanting to the paintings in progress. I would move continually about the huge dark interior, watching each painting being made, sometimes questioning the painter about his color and intent – why the board was of a certain kind or size, and so on.

I recall Kaapa was often in the painting room much earlier than the other men, for he was a kind of guardian of the place and he normally had the key. He did not trust the white staff of the Papunya settlement; he often told me how he thought they were thieves and liars and that the safety of the paintings was therefore very important. In his robust way he would tell me of his utter contempt for the whites as people. Most of the painting men felt that the white people were insincere, but Kaapa was aware of their capacity for brutality and abject force in dealing with blacks. He knew at first hand the mockery they had shown towards his own work before 1971, and he had not forgotten his humiliation.

A tall, splendid-looking fellow named Tim Leura came to the painting room early one morning in February 1972 and asked whether I had board and paints that he could use that day. I asked why he hadn't come forward earlier and he said, 'I've been watching you.' He was very quiet during his first day's work in the painting room. He painted for about ten hours and produced 'Bush Tucker Story'. It was sent, as far as I know, to Harry Giese's government collection in Darwin and I have not seen it since. Tim, who was to become my closest friend at Papunya, waited for me at the end of the day. I said, 'You're a good painter'; but Tim knew very well that he was much more than a good painter and he just said, rather matter-of factly, 'I haven't got any money.' I gave him $10, which was all I had, and I recall how Tim just looked at me searchingly, adjusted his great bush hat, chuckled and whispered, 'You're a real boss.' Tim Leura was very quickly to become one of the great painters at Papunya and also my valued helper and intermediary, together with Kaapa, Yala Yala and Bill Stockman.

A few days later I came to the painting room early and saw a dusty, wild-haired man with a squinting eye whom I'd not seen before. He had lost one eye and his eyebrow had closed over the socket. His name was Clifford Possum Tjapaltjarri and he was very untidy and dusty. He had already found a board and was at work. Tim spoke for him: 'This is my brother, Clifford. I can't beat him. (Tim Leura often spoke of 'beating' other people in his painting and his career as

31

a stockman. In conversation with the men we would often joke that Shorty Lungkata was 'beating' Uta Uta today, and so on, about the Pintupi or Anmatjira Aranda having a good day.) I made Clifford welcome and he worked away with zest just like the other painters. Clifford's first painting was of an 'Emu Corroboree Man'.

It was my practice to go hunting with the men and I soon realized that the tails were the most prized part of the kangaroo. After each hunting I trip I would collect the tails and take them to the older men, who greatly liked the offerings. One time I left the tails in my car overnight and the next morning they were gone. I went to the painting room and complained to the men that someone had stolen my tails. At least ten of the men went to my quarters and carefully searched the vehicle and surrounding grass and soil for tracks and other evidence. Eventually they went into a great huddle, which took some time. Then they searched again and went into another huddle. Finally three of the men declared that they had satisfied themselves that the tails had been taken not by a human but by dogs.

I had the feeling that they were trying to say something else, but I let it go at that. I was interested in how they let their group loyalties come through and how, in their patient and quiet and infinitely courteous way, they could speak *to* me and yet at the same time *past* me, because I was not one of them and never could be.

Occasionally, after a few hours' painting, I would take some of the painters out to the airstrip to give driving lessons. Most of the men had an idea of how to drive on bush tracks, but town and highway driving was another matter. It was terribly important to them to get a licence. On weekends, when I could be available all day, four, five, six or seven of us would pile into my combi and go off to the airstrip. The airstrip at Papunya was about three kilometres from the settlement, flanked by spinifex and sandhills, and was used by the small planes bringing mail and supplies from Alice Springs. I was almost never out there to see planes, but rather to drive up and down the runway with the painters.

Most were slow to learn and none of them got licences while I was there, although there may have been another reason for this. The police actively discouraged Aboriginal men from having driving licences so that they could be stopped and charged on their way into or out of Alice Springs.

I had to take the men to Papunya police station for their written or oral exams. I remember Kaapa being asked by a policeman, 'What do you do after a car accident?' Kaapa called out, in his characteristically quick style, 'Go to sleep.' And then he was asked, 'What do you do if you have too much to drink?' Again his answer was 'Go to sleep.' He had a point.

The painting, not unlike the hunting and the driving, was always a joyous coming together and celebration by the painters – of each other and of me. We were a kind of society in which all of these activities were symbols of friendship.

One Sunday afternoon, after a most intense morning of painting, Kaapa and Mick Namerari were working side by side, enormously preoccupied with their work. Although I was quite tired I remember being persuaded, against my better judgement, to take Nosepeg and Old Mick Tjakamarra with some petrol to a car which Nosepeg told me had broken down on the Haast's Bluff Road. We set off in my combi into the hot dusty afternoon and I soon realized that I had not been told what the real distance was. The car was nowhere to be seen but we had gone too far to turn back. I became tense and angry with Nosepeg and Old Mick and yet they didn't seem to mind. They had both been drinking that day and were very jolly.

We had gone more than eighty kilometres along the road before I realized that someone had walked to Papunya to bring the news that the car wouldn't go. As we went along, Nosepeg was sick in the car and the smell of it added to our discomfort in the heat and dust. When at last I got to the rusted heap by the roadside I was greeted by six drunken men madly flagging me down. The car had run out of petrol, all right, but it was a 'flagon wagon' – used to bring alcohol to the outpost – and all of the men waiting were badly drunk. I did not leave the petrol but went straight back to Papunya, leaving everyone waving nonchalantly behind me.

In the late twilight I returned to the painting room, since Kaapa had asked me to lock up that day. There against the galvanized-iron wall were two paintings which Kaapa and Mick Namerari had been working on when I left. Mick had done a children's story, 'Naughty Boys' Sweet Lollies', and Kaapa had done a 'Rainbow Water Dreaming'. The paintings greeted me like a kind of gift, for they were masterpieces of their subject, quite extraordinarily original in treatment and of great gentleness and beauty.

It was as though these two had made their painting that day as a means of saying something to me only. As I gazed in wonder through the strange blue light of that empty place, I was suddenly filled with a great joy and I simply saw the paintings in all their glory, and nothing else.

Finding an Outlet

I had bought several paintings for myself and was authorized by Fred Friis to buy a collection for the school. This was conceived as a museum collection, and a companion to the murals, for the benefit of the Papunya Aborigines.

In August an early work by Kaapa Tjampitjinpa was entered in the Caltex Art Competition in Alice Springs. It won equal first prize with a work by a European artist. Kaapa's success in Alice Springs, and the vast number of paintings being produced, led me to take a selection to town for sale. My teaching assistant, Obed Raggett, announced this at a meeting in the art room. The Pintupi were with the other painting men for the first time and there was frantic excitement. That weekend, over \$1300 cash was raised from the sale of paintings. It was a sensation at Papunya. The Aboriginal men were jubilant. At least five large cash sales were made during the following months, involving some six hundred paintings by twenty-five men.

I was still a class art teacher at the Papunya school and there was no time allocation or work obligation on my part to sell the Papunya paintings in Alice Springs or assist the Aboriginal men in any way. Painting, however, was a shared interest between the men and myself, and the seriousness of these mature-age men, as well as their determined attitude, induced me to help them.

From pondering the various drawings and designs I came to know the styles of individual painters. I learned that, below the superficial detail, there was a wonderful repertoire of motifs and patterns which could be used in many combinations to tell a story about some animal, bird or place – which the men would describe as 'my Dreaming' or 'my country'. The motif for a star, then the signs for running water, a man, groups of men at a place, all became known to me. Obed Raggett's capabilities in translation, and general assistance when paintings were sold, were of great value, and together we drew annotated diagrams to decipher for potential buyers the abstract arrangements in the paintings.

Although I did not take any commission on sales I became a kind of 'agent' for the painters. My relationship developed into something like that between the owner of an art gallery and an artist, my role being to interpret the paintings for the public and to relay feedback to the artist.

The painters often used secret-sacred designs but abandoned them when they realized that this might cause controversy. They were amused because I did not want to know any of the secrets behind such designs, for all I wanted was for them to produce non-controversial work that would earn them good money. I construed the changed rules of secrecy as a change in the relationship between the Aboriginal people and me.

I was fascinated by the graphic symbols and motifs used, and their validity as simplifications of perceived objects. I did not want these to be changed, and advised against 'whitefella' elements or themes.

Following Kaapa's success I applied myself to raising technical standards in the painting, 'clarifying' the mythology and generally encouraging the men who responded willingly to this.

When attempting to lift the spirits of the Aboriginal painters I would ask for 'good paintings to beat the white fellow painter'. During the day's work I would talk endlessly to the painting men, repeating my advice on how to do good work, how to beat the white painters in town, how to 'catch' the big men with good work, and talk like that. Results came from such encouragement.

By my insisting on slow, careful work with good stories, the men developed an inspired concentration. They understood the advice not to use any signs or colors that were 'whitefella'. There was pressure on them to do it well. Anything that is excellent is 'pala lingo' – 'flash' in pidgin English – and they understood this requirement. Careless work or something unfinished would be singled out and denounced.

It pleased me that the painters depended on me to do the story diagrams for them. The paintings could not really be sold until this was done, and the men cheerfully came to me for this about the time the picture was nearly finished. Despite the language barrier (often they would help each other) they responded to any praise I would give them. My attitude of course affected the price, since I valued the paintings also. So the recording of the stories was an important ceremony which they enjoyed. Here was a white man wanting to help, who was much accepted by the community and was really getting the Aborigines that most precious of things: money. To them it was 'big' money and we had long talked of buying a truck like the celebrated red truck of the Pintupi, with Kaapa Tjampitjinpa always eager to get another vehicle.

The Aborigines were always very enthusiastic if the word was put around that a certain white person would pay money for their paintings or artefacts. When I made it known that I was starting a collection of my own many men approached me. The watercolor artists Keith Namatjira and Joshua Ebatarintja, both Aranda men from Hermannsburg, had married local women and had children at the 'special' school. Papunya was their home. In a very short time these men also became known to me.

In October 1971 I arranged for the Papunya Artists' Co-operative to be formed within the Papunya School. This organization was bitterly resented by the administration since, as part of the school, it was outside their control. The formation of the co-operative owed nothing at all to the government policies at that time and was in fact in opposition to Commonwealth government policies, which aimed at terminating Aboriginal traditional life, culture and languages. Fred Friis was treasurer, and made cash payments to the men at 'pay times'. The Welfare Branch of the Department of the Interior, which administered Papunya, had then wanted an exclusively white company to govern the activities of the painting men, but the Aboriginal men told me that they wanted their own company, without the hated Welfare Branch. I insisted that an Aboriginal name be used for the company and there followed a series of appalling and savage exchanges with the administration officers. I was reminded that I was 'still a white man', and that if I presumed to behave otherwise my future work at the outpost would be at risk.

The name 'Papunya Tula' was born at a gathering with some painters at Charley Creek in Alice Springs in June 1972. I recall saying that morning, 'What do you want to call the company?' With me were two Pintupi men, Charlie Tarawa (Tjaruru) and Mick Namerari Tjapaltjarri, and one Anmatjira Aranda, Tim Leura. Charlie Tarawa (Tjaruru) blurted out, as if he'd known all his life, 'Papunya Tula'. (The term 'Papunya Tula' refers specifically to the smaller of two hills not far from Papunya and means 'a meeting place for all brothers and cousins'. It is a Honey Ant Dreaming site shared equally by all traditional Aboriginal groups in Central Australia and the Western Desert region.) Then I asked, 'Does that keep all the mobs happy?' Everyone said, 'Yes, yes, yes,' that it did very much; and that morning Papunya Tula became a living idea, and everyone was very happy.

Friends

One of my most vivid memories of Papunya was a breathlessness of bodies rushing across the red dust of the settlement courtyard, then up the steps into the low-ceilinged cement court house, and a police sergeant yelling to Kaapa and the other men to halt. They had passed the sacred honey ant tree which was in the police grounds next to the court, and the sergeant could be heard shouting, 'Come on, now now, come on, come on, move,' as the tall, ragged black men ran barefoot and wildly past. Another group of dejected black men squatted in the shade near the tree, waiting to be called, hardly talking, unless in a sort of blank reply to a remark that had not been made.

This was autumn 1972. Kaapa Tjampitjinpa had been called up before the police court convened at the Papunya settlement in the Western Desert. The settlement authorities considered him an incorrigible drunk and an unsettling influence. A deputy superintendent had told me that day that this particular Kaapa was to be deported to Yuendumu because of his drinking and that if I interfered I would be removed from Papunya as well. The cautioner was a small, tough, muscular man who'd been made even tougher in New Guinea, and his approach to black men was all cautionary, brutal directness. You could hear him in the evenings outside his house giving Tarzan screams and beating his chest, as his predecessor had, so that his incantations echoed up and down the white Papunya streets.

Kaapa was not as tall as many of the Anmatjira Aranda but he was very quick to see what others might not see at all. (I often thought he saw far too much, and perhaps this was why he drank more than he should.) He always moved in a fast, deft spring-walk, intense and convoluted as he whispered in his strange, pressed-together, mixed-up English. 'Chep,' he'd whisper (for Geoff). 'Chep, Chep, can you help me, can you get new wood off-cuts for paints, Chep?' And whenever I could I'd say, 'Yes, yes, I will, Kaap, yes.'

Kaapa was very bright, but very down to earth as well, an extraordinary survivor in a despairing environment. I remember him particularly for his intense way of seeming to be everywhere at all times, doing things mysteriously and well. He was always travelling out of Papunya, to Yuendumu or Alice Springs or myriad other places. For his trouble with his earlier paintings he had been derided by the whites in Alice Springs, until he won the leading art prize. And he wasn't a tidy man and he didn't shave for weeks on end. As he sprang towards you he looked for all the world like a two-legged human swag. He drank a great deal and a Kaapa hangover was something everyone in the camps seemed to share.

On that brilliant, blue-skied morning in autumn the wind was cold at the Papunya court house. The Aboriginal men, shadow-like and all dismay, seemed spent as their names were mockingly yelled out by the court orderly and sometimes the police sergeant. If they did not run immediately they were screamed at again. The men would stand listless or lost-away while charges of drunkenness were called out and they nodded, yes, yes, yes. They always agreed with what was said about them because they knew that was why they had been rushed into the courtroom. Sometimes there were more men than charges read, as often days and times were confused. Perhaps Bill Stockman would be there, and the magistrate would smile ironically and say, 'You're not here today, Bill, we don't need you.' And Bill Stockman, another of the great painters, would trot from the room like a two-legged dog and the magistrate and the court would try not to laugh.

That day Kaapa was mumbling in strange fractions of words, standing lost-away before this European magistrate who called him Kaapa, an easy version of his real name. The settlement official addressed the magistrate sternly and authoritatively and said that this wretched Kaapa must be deported from the camp with or without his family because he was an unsettling influence. He drinks, he disregards the law, he is not a nice fellow, he upsets the administration. It is all very ironic and sad in the court, especially the way the Aboriginal drunks cannot or do not want to speak the English language at all. But the magistrate drones on in spite of this sadness and the black men run in and out.

Then the court adjourned and Kaapa sat in the long grass with me. He was distressed and he said, 'Chep, Chep, I do not want to go to Yuendumu. You help me,' but the words all came out at once. I said, 'All right, I will.' We went back into the court after the adjournment and I told the magistrate that Kaapa Tjampitjinpa was a most brilliant painter whose loss from the settlement would be a great blow to Aboriginal culture. He was actually allowed to stay at Papunya. I said to the magistrate later, 'Come down to the painting room. There's some important work going on there. You can see what I'm talking about.' He actually came. He was quite a nice fellow. And Kaapa could stay at home.

Kaapa had a certain toughness, an intransigence, and he tended not to explain his work the way his good friend Johnny Warrangkula did. He was significantly dispassionate about his work being sold, whereas the Pintupi and most of the other artists, even Tim Leura, were concerned in the early days about where their paintings went. Most of the artists felt there was a quality of immortality about their paintings, yet Kaapa seemed quite wilfully to paint sacred objects and disdained any immortality from the start.

Johnny Warrangkula was Kaapa's best friend but, interestingly, a very different kind of man. He was rather slower than Kaapa, and he seemed, in his quiet, gentle, patient way, to be the friend of everyone he met. He used mainly earth colors in his work and he was one of the great Papunya masters. Somehow, subtly, I felt you knew Kaapa better if you knew Johnny. Gentleness, perhaps, has no bounds.

In April 1972 I was in Alice Springs with Johnny and we were on a street corner. Johnny had had a pronounced stutter since he was a child, and on this day he was rebuking his son Sabin for energetic drinking. As he stuttered and waved his hands two young policemen came up and silently began to arrest men around us and force them into a panel van. They grabbed Johnny, too, and pushed him towards the van. I was upset and complained that he wasn't drunk. They ignored me, smirking, and pushed Johnny into the van. He spent the weekend in gaol and on the Monday the Alice Springs court convened. A question was asked of the policemen giving evidence: was Johnny upset? The policeman said, 'No, he wasn't, only the man with the camera.' This man was me.

I remember very well how at all times Johnny was like a lamb and had no hostility towards anyone, how he did not know that day what he was convicted of because he spoke very little English. In court I came forward and told the magistrate that Johnny had not been drinking and that he had a bad stutter. The magistrate said, 'Convicted, cautioned and discharged.' I don't think Johnny Warrangkula understood one word of what was said in court that day, except perhaps his name.

One of the most interesting ways to get to know the Aboriginal men was to collect wood for fires. Kaapa often asked me to go with him some way from Papunya so as to get firewood for himself, Mick Namerari and Johnny Warrangkula, his close friends. Papunya and much of the countryside about had long been stripped bare of its firewood for there were too many people living in too small an area. There was dust everywhere in the settlement and it gave the children chest illnesses, respiratory complaints and runny noses.

'Chep, Chep,' Kaapa would say, Johnny Warrangkula by his side, looking dreamily at you from under his bush hat, 'poor firewood, Chep.' And he'd murmur quickly about how we should go to get it, which we would then do. Out we'd go in my trusty combi along lonely cross-country tracks I'd never seen before and would never see again, Kaapa and Mick and Johnny sitting there, seeming to wave at some special trees or rock as we bounced wildly along. We'd go quite some distance out and Kaapa would select a tree, calling to his son Bobby or his other children or Mick or Johnny. He'd say 'Chep' and I'd drive my combi at the tree, probably hundreds of years old and now dead, and snap it down. Then we would all collect the broken wood and put it in my van. Collecting the wood was a gentle but endless business, as only long-dead trees would be selected, leaving the living ones where they were.

It seemed that each person at Papunya had a fire – each child, the mother, the father. They were not large fires, but small and constantly glowing or smoking, day and night. These small, sociable fires would dot the Papunya glade and I would often share with my friends the feeling that a fire could bring. In a quiet and humble way I was taking part in their culture, as though I were one of them.

When we'd collected the wood, we'd drive back towards Papunya through wild and (to me) unmarked and uncharted spinifex and acacia desert until we saw again the concrete-and-steel transitional huts, barbaric and hideously ugly, with a few vestigial black figures in dusty clothes moving solemnly about. (Though some Aborigines tried to co-operate with the authorities by living in the huts, mostly they found them alien and confining, and used them as urinals and lavatories. I suppose it was a way of telling us what they thought of us.)

When I was teaching at the school the children were often taken outside to work on slates and when they were finished they untidily left the slates where they were. Sometimes these slates would vanish, as if spirited away and the same evening, as if by the same magic, Kaapa would bring me a marvellous painting on a school slate, smiling quite unapologetically and saying, 'Chep, would you like this one?' His roguish look said, 'Well, we know each other so well by now that we are past apologizing.' Off he would go, whistling like the budgerigar that was his Dreaming, with the money I had paid him but could ill afford.

On one occasion in 1972 Kaapa came to me and said, all at once, in his special way, that his car had broken down and could I help him go and get it now. But he was vague about where it had broken down, muttering something about 'towards next town'. Kaapa's mates, Mick Namerari and Johnny Warrangkula, came along as well, and on the way we passed many large clay pans filled with water. We stopped a few times and Mick Namerari got out and had a shot at the ducks in the shallows; but he had the wrong sort of gun that day, and he missed. As usual, Kaapa and Mick and Johnny talked laconically to the country as we ripped along through the red or grey dust. By the time we reached the Beef Road to Yuendumu, Kaapa's car was in sight, but it had taken an extraordinary turn for the worse. It seemed to have lost everything but its shape.

Kaapa was terribly serious as he walked round and round his car, looking at where the engine, bonnet, lights, grill, steering wheel, spare tyre and wheels had been. Yet he wasn't angry; just quietly sad. Mick and Johnny stood by with great solemnity while Kaapa continued to walk round his wretched car which looked like a kind of exotic plant or seed. Then he halted and scratched his wild, unruly hair. 'Chep, this was metal scrap dealer, not other fella,' he murmured to me. 'Chep, car registered,' he whispered, while Mick and Johnny watched, shocked, not speaking. 'Not good, Chep. Not good. Cannot do this to registered car, Chep, cannot.' And a few moments later he began whistling.

On the way back, Mick and Johnny had a go at a few more ducks; but everything was like Kaapa's car – it just got away – and it was well after dark when we arrived back at Papunya. Kaapa went to the police to complain about his car, but they took no notice of him and many things went unsaid. Of course, the police never did take action for Aborigines. Kaapa told me later that he had only lent the car to a cousin when it became dead, since he didn't have a licence himself to drive. This was Kaapa Tjampitjinpa, the master painter of Papunya, that fellow who, it was said, drank, talked and questioned things and had once been found with someone else's paint brushes in his hand. He was more than doubly unlucky, and I believe he knew this very well.

At the end of our journey, when the car came to a halt, I pretended to be handcuffed. Johnny began to chuckle and he couldn't stop. He chuckled and roared, which was startling because he was a painter of almost unrelieved gravity and I had thought everything was serious to Johnny. Then Kaapa began to laugh, and so did I. And all about handcuffs. It was very good to laugh with such marvellous fellows at that time and in that place. At such times I did not think of the men as painters at all, but only as dear and wondrous friends.

A Winter of Bitterness and Loss

I had seen the first painting sales as a source of hope for Aboriginal people. There had been a terrible lack of dignity and self-esteem in the black men, and the money they were earning made me believe that much of this would change, if only the people could stand up and be themselves. The painting movement had brought forth an enormous passion in the desert people to develop their own style and their own sense of self. In a way they were being freed, and redeeming themselves and their culture, by their creativeness.

The painting men were quite pleased with themselves. I bought them thirty new army hats, and they kept their brushes in their hatbands. Hunting and food gathering became lyric adventures for me and I was happy indeed. Since I planned to stay one more year, I applied for, and was given, a cultural grant to continue my work. If we just kept working, superlative standards might be reached.

However, towards the end of the first school year certain events began to trouble me. It was suggested that I was trafficking in paintings from a government Aboriginal reserve. It seemed that the new superintendent intended to stop me doing this work for the Aboriginal men. Certain actions were taken against me and private letters were opened. Some letters were intercepted by the post office and never delivered. I had every reason to believe that I was being investigated by ASIO and I felt I was a marked man. In January 1972 I was forbidden to leave the outpost on weekdays without permission from the Alice Springs welfare office. I applied to go to town on a particular Thursday.

I was extremely worried as I prepared my combi for the four-hundred-kilometre return journey. I recall it took me all night to label and describe fifty paintings and jam them into my van. Old Walter arrived at 4 a.m. and helped carry the rest of the paintings.

The superintendent had indicated that the paintings were by 'government Aborigines' and therefore were 'government paintings'. I did not underestimate his threat to prevent me selling the work. The Aboriginal culture, to my mind, was being terminated and this new achievement had to be brought to the attention of the nation. I was away by 5.30 and I felt as though I was running guns through some kind of frontier or security force. I saw the personal ambitions of the superintendent and the racist police as provocative, and I sensed a certain danger in the whole enterprise.

The bush roads were very hard on my light truck and corrugations shook the load mercilessly. My predicament made me very afraid. I took the paintings to the gallery and left them as a consignment, not for cash sale as had been the case until then. It was a huge relief to get the work out of Papunya and I felt I had done something worthwhile for Aboriginal liberty. When I returned to the outpost later that day I called a meeting of all the painting men and the school committee with Obed Raggett as translator. I explained what I had done and that the painters would receive their money after the holidays.

Many of the staff of Papunya and people in Alice Springs had already begun to shun me, and I felt, outside of my circle of Aboriginal friends and a few others, very much alone. The coup de grâce was delivered by the administration when I was away from the settlement. In my absence a representative went with the storeman to the painting room to make a dispersal of money. The men were told, with crude gestures, that there was $21 left for them from the $700 sale because the rest had been deducted as expenses. And that was all.

The monies for the painters, I found later, had been deliberately held back. The Aboriginal painters were often couriers for the money from Alice Springs, and Tim Leura told me that the money was among the parcels he delivered to the settlement authorities. The so-called expenses to the painters, which effectively would deprive them of income for some time, were enormous quantities of masonite and wood. The administration was ordering materials in this quantity without consulting me and thereby making the painters clients and creditors of the Welfare Branch.

The men knew better than to express too openly their feelings about the administration. Since the riot in April of that year there had been increasingly heavy-handed attempts to demoralize the black people. I remember very well the sight of Johnny Warrangkula and Tim Leura at my door, both of them looking almost grotesquely agitated, Johnny stuttering and whispering and trembling, trying to tell me about the 'no money'. Tim was dreadfully sullen, and once the story was told, he whispered, 'No more buy on credit.' Tim knew very well the way the cattle station owners turned the Aboriginal stockmen into hopeless dependants by extending credit, and he did not want it. He hated it.

I remember the Pintupi presenting themselves dismally to me in the great painting room, the scene of their earlier and incomparable triumphs, the group no longer happy or cohesive. The painting men were now in a 'great worry', for my promise of good money for good work had been broken. Obed Raggett explained to the Pintupi men that the fault was not mine, but I was unconvinced for a long time that they believed him.

Tim Leura often explained to me the attitude of the men and assisted me greatly in my dealings with them. By now I had traded my gun, clothes and radio for paintings. To create support and a cash flow for the men, I seemed to be selling or giving away everything I owned. Sensing the impending end of my work with the men, I strove harder and harder. If I had not acted with such vigorous intent, the Papunya Tula movement could have been smothered at birth. It was during this time of anguish that I realized I had to get the paintings out of Papunya as fast as I could. In addition to the six hundred-odd paintings I had sold in Alice Springs, I had sold about three hundred to various interested persons and, by a sort of default, built a personal collection of more than a hundred paintings. This meant that about a thousand paintings had been produced to date, in defiance of the Commonwealth government policies that were destroying Aboriginal culture. I felt I was making a point about the esteem owed to Aboriginal culture, yet I was undermined by bureaucrats and art dealers.

I seemed to find it much harder to communicate with the painters after that first demand for money and, though I was still liked, I knew somehow everything had changed. While the men were painting, I had witnessed the sense of the glory that the Aboriginal people bring forth in their ceremonies and dances and songs. Now there seemed to me only the stale, sick stench of the camps, the awful physical nearness of the used-up sand, the filth, and the destitution of the alcoholic faces about the tracks and streets. These ragged, dirty settlement bands of Aboriginal people seemed more and more like some terrible travesty of what they had once been and there seemed now nothing I could do to help. What reputation I had, I began to feel was now being taken from me by stealth by the authorities.

There was a quality of fantasy about those declining days, in the way there seemed so little substance now in anything I could do or say. I became sick, and the Aboriginal men would come and knock on my door to ask me how I was. I would say very little as they stood there awkwardly and murmured about Kaapa or Clifford or someone else who wasn't there. I would sometimes say to them, 'Yes, there is something I will do. Yes, there is perhaps some way I can help you. You will truly get your money.' And yet I could do nothing.

It was in the painting shed itself that the final blow came. The painters were waiting for me, surrounded by paintings half-completed or just begun. There must have been as many as forty men there that day in June 1972 and when I came in they threw their paints and brushes on the sand. They would not paint, they said. Nor could I prevail upon them to paint without money. The monstrousness of it was not lost on me as they began to chant in their own languages amongst themselves, then at me: 'Money, money, money.'

I recall how the painting room interior was heavy with fine red dust, and how flies swarmed feverishly about each time the door to the painting room opened and another painter came in. The men were standing about, cursing and muttering. Then Charlie Tarawa (Tjaruru) came over to me, obviously sent by the other Pintupi, and yelled, 'What about this fucking money, boss, what about fucking money?' He was speaking on this occasion for the Pintupi, the magnificent free men of the Gibson Desert, and I was distressed by what he said. As the men murmured now in their own languages, very quickly and quite unintelligibly, it seemed that I was becoming quite separate from them and, in a way, even from myself.

Yet at that very moment the Aboriginal painters had conceptualized a new art form. On the canvases and boards at Papunya something was being made that had never been seen before. But as the door was just about to open onto this new world there was talk about money and nothing else, and so it seemed to me that the journey was ending just as quickly as it had begun.

Tim Leura was the still, calm centre I had to hang onto as 1972 moved into winter and I began to understand what our society, even through me, was doing to the painting men. Tim was forever counselling me about the importance to the men of the money brought into the community by the sale of the paintings. Yet this money, it had become painfully apparent to me, and the obsession for it, were as much a sickness in the interior deserts as anywhere else.

(After I left Papunya great revenge was taken against Tim Leura because he had been an outstanding spokesman and he was my close friend. This was the white way. Tim was put down, not all at once, but slowly, over a number of years. I believe that they tried to make him feel they were helping him each time they gave a cut, and of course he knew what they were doing.)

From my window I'd see strange and wistful caravans of black faces coming back and forth along the spinifex tracks. I'd see someone I thought was one of the painters, and then whoever it was would walk away. It was finished, truly finished, I knew; and I drove out of Papunya in July 1972 with a despair and a fury I had never known before, towards Alice Springs, for I had truly lost the game.

I arrived in Alice Springs in a kind of fever and told the administration what I thought of them. Then I resigned and the officers did not seem to care what I did or where I went.

I woke a few days later in a hospital bed. Tim and Johnny and Mick Namerari and the other painters were standing in the ward and in the corridors, just whispering and nodding and not seeming to talk about anything but just being there. Sometimes when I'd wake up again I'd see Mick with Tim or Kaapa or Johnny W. There was a strange distant closeness about everything that was said, in spite of ordinary words not being used at all, and about the men, all quiet and gesturing with hands and faces.

On the Sunday morning, when I stepped into the hospital corridor, I was confronted with the sight of eight of the painters, with broken legs or arms all bloody, staring at me from outside the casualty ward. They had been in a wild and vicious fight in town the night before and now they were being repaired. They looked very lost in their loose, blood-stained bandages, but I suppose the tiredness was what I noticed most. We didn't say much and I just sat with them for what seemed a long time, inspecting their arms and legs and blackened eyes. I asked them about our beloved painting room. Was it all right? Did Kaapa still have the key, so the white buggers couldn't get in? They smiled very nicely at that, for it was a well-known joke amongst us. Then I remember them in ones and twos slipping away from where I sat watching on a chair by the entrance, and sort-of smiling and stumbling across the hospital front to the streets. I saw them become somehow quite unknown to me in the hot wind dazzling the lawns under the hospital trees. Soon the painters were further along the open, empty, ugly Alice Springs streets and then they were gone.

My brother flew into Alice Springs that day to find me, and two days later we flew out of there and I returned to Sydney, only to enter another hospital. But even to speak of it now would be like living that time all over again; so the story will not be told, for it cannot.

THE ARTISTS AND THEIR WORK

O F THE TWENTY-ODD MEN eventually painting full-time at Papunya in 1971–72, eight produced particularly interesting results. They were Tim Leura Tjapaltjarri, Kaapa Tjampitjinpa, Clifford Possum Tjapaltjarri, Tim Payungka Tjapangati, Mick Namerari Tjapaltjarri, Charlie Tarawa (Tjaruru) Tjungurrayi, Old Walter Tjampitjinpa and Johnny Warrangkula Tjupurrula. Their work is featured and discussed here in a sequence which reflects the development of the painting movement as a whole. (All works illustrated are acrylic on composition board, unless otherwise stated.)

Two Pintupi men at work in the painting room.

PHOTOGRAPH: ALLAN SCOTT

Old Walter Tjampitjinpa at Papunya in 1971 with his wife (now deceased).

OLD WALTER TJAMPITJINPA One Christmas, after I had been transporting the paintings for almost a year, I had occasion to prepare a consignment of work for Alice Springs. I had worked in my school art room all night and expected the painters to arrive in the morning to help me. Just before dawn I heard footsteps on the stairs. It was Old Walter, come to assist in wrapping up paintings. Aboriginal men like to wear long trousers to conceal their thin legs, but Old Walter was wearing shorts and cowboy boots, as he so often did. He worked for hours, helping and not saying a word.

One morning he and Old Bert Tjakamarra came late to the painting room, a little drunk and giggly. Old Walter apologised, saying he was 'sorry' for a recent death.

The painting men were all older than me, and I had great respect for them; but it was Old Walter for whom I felt a particularly strong affection. He spoke quietly, in a garbled, humble manner, yet he had a stupendous concentration that brought wonderful improvement to his painting skills.

Old Walter owned the Water Dreaming in his tribal society. It was his favourite subject, and most of his paintings are connected to the water spirit and the nourishment of bush tucker.

When, in 1980, I was finally told of Walter's blindness and nearness to death, I wanted to see him, and protect him with my coat, but Alice Springs was too far away by then.

Artist Old Walter Tjampitjinpa
Tribe Pintupi
Born c 1912 *Died* 1980
Story Water Dreaming at Kalipimpinpa
Completed 1971
Size 55 × 38 cm (house paint on board)
Location Kalipimpinpa
Custodian Tjampitjinpa-Tjangala

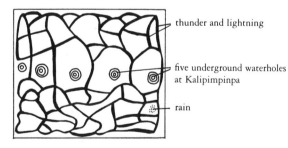

thunder and lightning

five underground waterholes
at Kalipimpinpa

rain

This is a brilliant interpretation of the landscape, a re-perception of the continent
with symbolic forms which may be called
hieroglyphs.

Artist Old Walter Tjampitjinpa
Tribe Pintupi
Born c 1912 *Died* 1980
Story Man's Water Dreaming
Completed 1971
Size 47 × 22 cm (poster paint & PVA on board)
Location Kalipimpinpa
Custodian Tjampitjinpa-Tjangala

The basic elements of the Water Dreaming are revealed in the U sign, the symbol for the waterman. The concentric circles represent the waterhole and the spiralling lines indicate water running across the sand. Old Walter was one of my close friends and he painted many variations on this water theme.

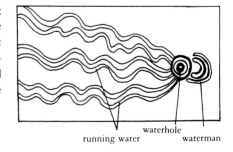

running water · waterhole · waterman

50

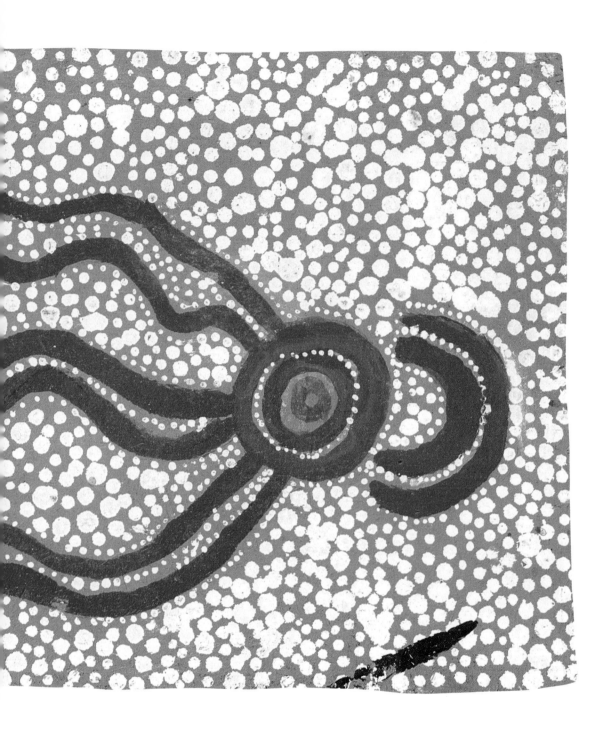

51

Johnny Warrangkula Tjupurrula, a leading Papunya painter, at work in the painting room, surrounded by his paintings.

PHOTOGRAPH: ALLAN SCOTT

JOHNNY WARRANGKULA TJUPURRULA was a village councillor when I first met him. He was quite forward in his dealings with white people and well known around the settlement. Johnny was a happy, expressive man with a slight stutter and tremor. He worked with intense concentration and had his own style. To overcome his difficulty with brushes he used extensive dotting and over-dotting, together with widely varied linear effects. His unique treatment held my attention and his work was very popular. I encouraged him to be different. Johnny was modest but exquisitely confident and proud, and loved having notes taken on the meaning of his work. He was almost condescending towards my painful efforts to understand his stories.

For Johnny, space outside the frame was the unseen and unfinished aspect of the painting. He would run off the frame, creating an irresolution of meaning and form, just as Clifford Possum created tension by perspective overlay.

Johnny's paintings are of major significance: they are strictly Aboriginal stories without conscious European influence, and yet they can be measured by the modern aesthetic. Although Johnny remained a 'primitive' on all grounds, he worked with great inventiveness outside the strict confines of totems and formal ritual. His work has anecdotal intimacy, a candid freshness and spontaneity that beguiles by its individuality. The use of dots in detailed ornament adds human expression. He uses calligraphic line with almost baroque excitement. Tight organization of bands and lines, hatching and dot embellishment give his work a powerful, energetic visual strength. He uses convoluted spiral symbols for people, and animal tracks and distorted figures as illustrations of ceremony – not in a formal way like Kaapa Tjampitjinpa, but intuitively.

Johnny fully understood that his paintings could be worth money in town and his output was prodigious. He would paint on anything, of any shape, length or size – even a matchbox. He would help me load my van and made sure he got plenty of his own paintings into it. Johnny kept his paintbrushes in his hat band. He referred to himself as one of the 'painting mob'. Kaapa was his best friend and there was just a little roguishness between the two of them. They were always after a car that would go to town, or at least to Glen Helen, where they could buy some liquor. These adventures usually failed because of poor cars or fighting.

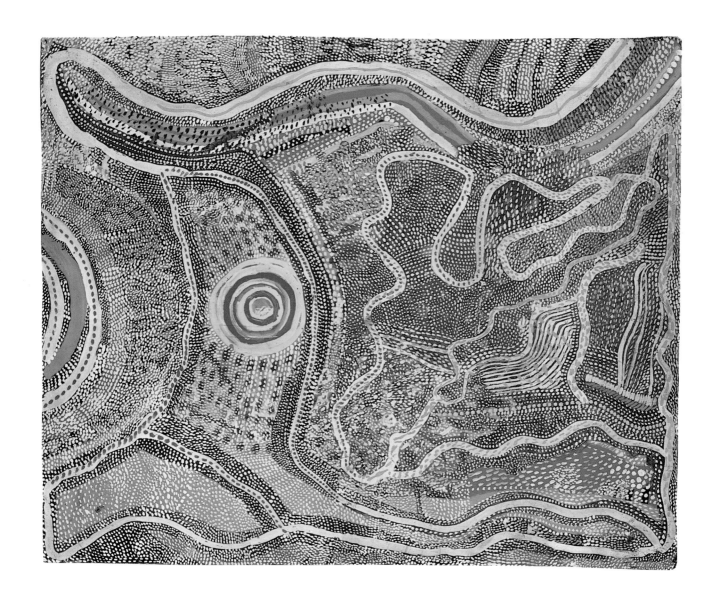

Artist Johnny Warrangkula Tjupurrula
Tribe Loritja
Born c 1932
Story Water Dreaming with Rain and Lightning
Completed 1972
Size 50 × 60 cm
Location Tjikari, north of Sandy Blight Junction, Western Australia
Custodian Tjupurrula-Tjakamarra

This calligraphic Water Dreaming includes all of the classic motifs connected with the fundamental Aboriginal story of rain, lightning, cliffs, caves, waterholes and bush tucker. The artist has been wonderfully successful in unifying his story signs and controlling the order of the design. The concentric circles are the artist's homeland waterhole at Tjikari. Another Water Dreaming site is at Kalipimpinpa, where there are five interconnected waterholes, some even running underground (See page 49).

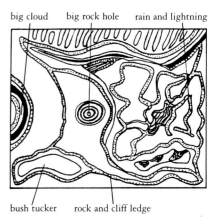

54

Artist Johnny Warrangkula Tjupurrula
Tribe Loritja
Born c 1932
Story Man and Naughty Boys' Water
Dreaming
Completed 1972
Size 50 × 60 cm
Location Kalipimpinpa, north-west of Sandy
Blight Junction, Western Australia
Custodian Tjupurrula-Tjakamarra

This painting is a variant of Mick Namerari's
'Naughty Boys' Dreaming'. In profile and
proportion the figure centre right is a corroboree man, his arms raised, chasing away
the four smaller figures of boys. The sinuous
lines represent water and cliffs near the rock
hole, which is indicated by concentric circles. The calligraphic detail and dotting
mean that this is a 'big place', where young
people are not allowed. The high tonal key,
the rich stippling and effervescent forms
make this an impressive example of Johnny
Warrangkula's work.

naughty boys

rock hole   old man

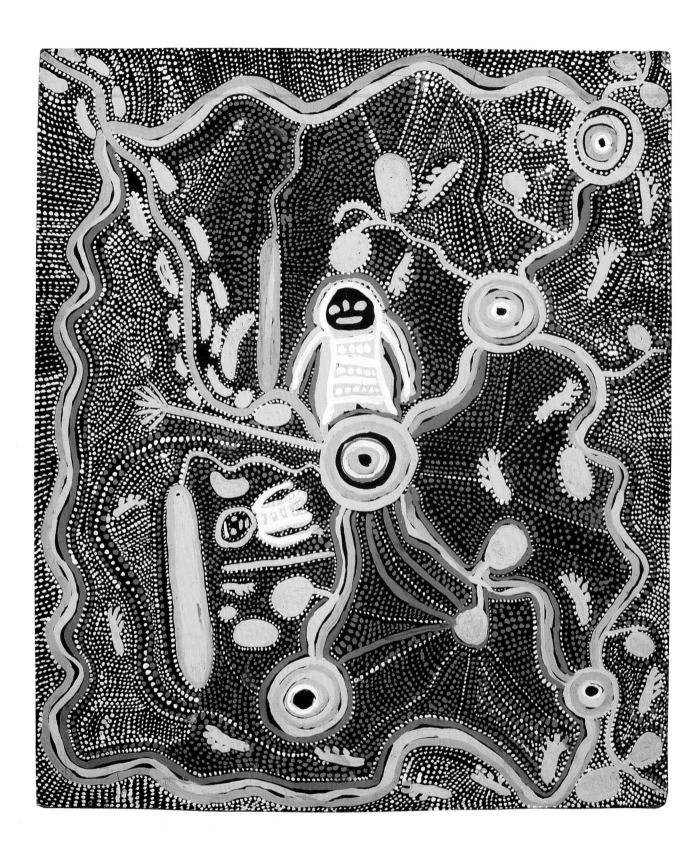

Detail Mother with tracks.

Artist Johnny Warrangkula Tjupurrula
Tribe Loritja
Born c 1932
Story Water Dreaming with Bush Tucker
Completed 1972
Size 50 × 40 cm (poster paint & PVA on board)
Location West of Papunya
Custodian Tjupurrula-Tjakamarra

This painting is unique in its inclusion of bullroarers, corroboree hats and tjurungas, which are disguised and therefore able to be seen by anybody. It is a fiction, referring to no particular people, place or journey tracks, although Dinny Nolan Tjampitjinpa has told me that the landscape is identifiable despite its being masked.

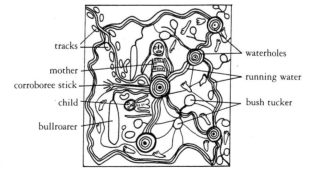

tracks
mother
corroboree stick
child
bullroarer
waterholes
running water
bush tucker

Artist Johnny Warrangkula Tjupurrula
Tribe Loritja
Born c 1932
Story Old Man's Story
Completed 1972
Size 24 × 54 cm (poster paint & PVA on board)
Location Tjikari, north of Sandy Blight Junction, Western Australia
Custodian Tjupurrula-Tjakamarra

Two old wallaby men are in a big cave near Tjikari in Tjupurrula's country. They sit by the fireplace indicated by concentric circles, with their spears, boomerangs and shields nearby. They are attacked by a large number of unfriendly old men who throw spears, boomerangs and stones. The frightened old men try to escape. The other old men give chase and catch them a long way from Tjikari, killing them and burying them in a big hole. This Dreaming is used for family entertainment.

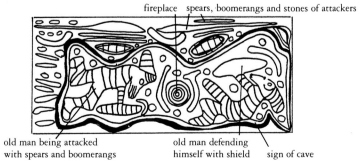

fireplace   spears, boomerangs and stones of attackers

old man being attacked
with spears and boomerangs

old man defending
himself with shield   sign of cave

Artist Johnny Warrangkula Tjupurrula
Tribe Loritja
Born c 1932
Story Bungalung Old Man's Fire Story
Completed 1972
Size 40 × 55 cm (poster paint & PVA on canvas)
Location Tjikari, north of Sandy Blight Junction, Western Australia
Custodian Tjupurrula-Tjakamarra

This story is connected to the Bushfire Dreaming of the wallaby people. An old man is looking about in the bush. He is called 'Bungalung' and is a giant. He is being chased by wallaby (*mala*) spirit people. Bungalung is caught by the rushing fire in the spinifex and the mulga. The pattern at the top of the painting shows where the fire has burnt through the grass and trees. Tracks show how the terrified old man has tried to escape. He runs a long way but the fire catches him. He calls out but he is trapped by the fire. He does not die straight away and is alive when the wallaby people find him. He dies later.

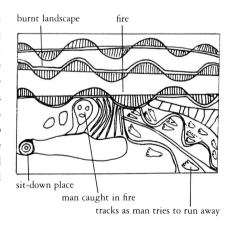

burnt landscape   fire

sit-down place
man caught in fire
tracks as man tries to run away

Long Jack Phillipus with family.

PHOTOGRAPH: ALLAN SCOTT

L ONG JACK PHILLIPUS TJAKAMARRA was very tall – at least 188 centimetres. Although strongly loyal to his Christian upbringing, he had a formidable tribal knowledge. He was a brilliant hunter and a good family man with five children. I first met Long Jack when he was one of the school yardmen (with Bill Stockman) responsible for the school murals. This was my first confrontation with questions of tribal and personal 'custody' of Dreamings and the issue of secrecy.

Artist Long Jack Phillipus Tjakamarra
Tribe Loritja
Born c 1935
Story Children's Kadaitcha Dreaming
Completed 1972
Size 35 × 56 cm (poster paint & PVA on board)
Location North-west of Sandy Blight Junction, Western Australia
Custodian Tjakamarra-Tjupurrula

The Kadaitcha man is one of the most feared aspects of tribal authority, having enormous power over life and death, and killing with great ferocity. He enforces Aboriginal law and punishment as decided by the old men in the community. However, the identity and activities of the Kadaitcha man are considered a mystery, and he wears special emu-feathered slippers to erase his own footprints.

In this story the Kadaitcha man has decapitated another man with a boomerang. Fires and smoke complete the story. This painting is remarkable in that it addresses this story for a general audience and includes a corroboree hat (modified from the traditional diamond).

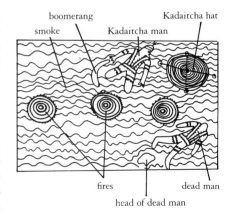

Artist Long Jack Phillipus Tjakamarra
Tribe Loritja
Born c 1935
Story Possum Dreaming
Completed 1975
Size 38 × 58 cm
Location North-west of Sandy Blight Junction, Western Australia
Custodian Tjakamarra-Tjupurrula

The centre concentric circles indicate fireplaces and those at either end of the journeys are the sit-down homes of the possum. The sets of stylized curving lines are the long journeys of the possum men. The spiral line that obliquely connects with the centre fireplaces is the track of the possum looking for food. The oval shapes are shields decorated with possum markings and the oblique bands represent body paint on the corroboree performers, who are indicated by the U shapes sitting at the concentric circles.

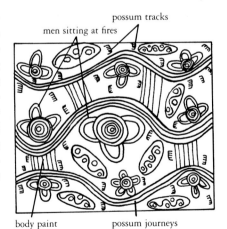

possum tracks
men sitting at fires
body paint
possum journeys

63

Old Tutuma Tjapangati at Papunya, 1971.

OLD TUTUMA TJAPANGATI, a very active pensioner, began borrowing painting equipment and working in my school art room when other pensioners, school yardmen and village councillors did so. Word of my availability spread through the Aboriginal community very quickly. Old Tutuma was an important ceremonial authority.

Artist Old Tutuma Tjapangati
Tribe Pintupi
Born c 1910 *Died* 1986
Story Old Men's Corroboree
Completed 1971
Size 54 × 100 cm (house paint on board)
Location West of Lake Macdonald, Western Australia
Custodian Tjapangati-Tjapananga-Tjangala-Tjampitjinpa

This simple Corroboree Dreaming shows a large group of men (indicated by circles) as ritual participants in a ceremony. The corroboree takes place on a big claypan shown by the large concentric circles. The weaving lines are the paths of the corroboree men as they move about the claypan preparing for the ceremonies. The men are seated around the corroboree stick, which is a specially erected pole. A man's shield is also shown, with a simple design on it. This is a very big family performance, with women and children also present. The old men are teaching the young people lessons which are part of the Tjingari cycles (See page 8).

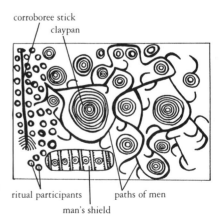

Artist Old Tutuma Tjapangati
Tribe Pintupi
Born c 1910 *Died* 1986
Story One Old Man's Dreaming
Completed 1971
Size 25 × 35 cm
Location West of Lake Macdonald, Western Australia
Custodian Tjapangati-Tjapananga-Tjangala-Tjampitjinpa

This Dreaming is a stylized map describing a very large area that is the artist's homeland, and only he can give details as to the places and ceremonial sites involved. The arrangement of concentric circles linked and surrounded by smaller ones, all representing special places, is usually painted as a sand mosaic. The straight lines represent travelling. The U sign top left is the corroboree man and the straight line beside him is his spear.

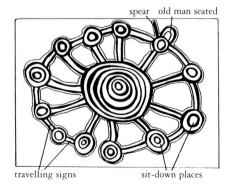

spear   old man seated

travelling signs   sit-down places

66

PHOTOGRAPH: ALLAN SCOTT

Old Mick Tjakamarra, the first important ceremonial man that I met.

OLD MICK TJAKAMARRA made himself known to me during the planning of the school murals. He and Tom Onion would bring Kaapa Tjampitjinpa to my school art room with sketches. He was very active for his age, and we often had lengthy discussions. Old Mick had a thin, quavering falsetto voice and spoke good English. Because he was such a good spokesman, I had little to do with the other men associated with the murals. By tribal custom and in conversation I was declared Old Mick's nephew. Old Mick is credited with belonging to the Anmatjira Aranda tribe, but he often described himself as 'mixed mob' – by which I assume he meant that either his father's marriages or his own had crossed with another tribal group, probably the Wailpri.

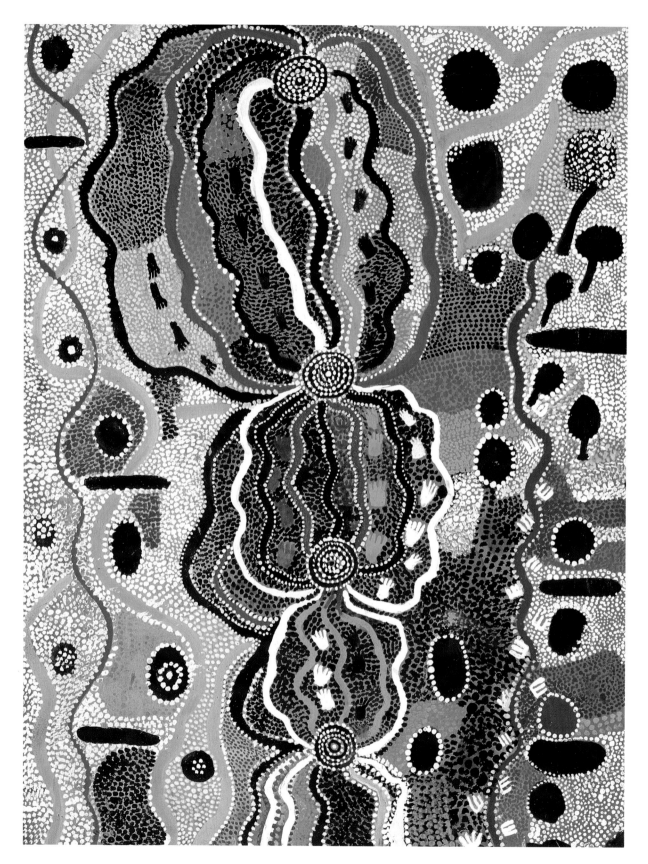

Detail Tracks of a boy looking for bush tucker.

Artist Old Mick Tjakamarra
Tribe Anmatjira Aranda
Born c 1910
Story Children's Water Dreaming with Possum Story
Completed 1973
Size 45 × 58 cm (poster paint & PVA on board)
Location Kutinyara, east of Mount Wedge
Custodian Old Mick as custodian for his father, Old Dan Bugger

This painting is one of the earlier appropriations of the dotting method used by Johnny Warrangkula to denote topography. Unlike Johnny, however, Old Mick used acrylic paints. Old Mick's technique is sometimes unfinished and rough, and the dotting is not a symmetrical arrangement but a means of converging the constituent areas.

The unself-conscious painterly quality of the work is due to the fact that Old Mick was not continuously involved in painting. This was one of his very few paintings and was developed slowly, the water passing like eternal thought over the desert sandhill surface held by four bull's-eye waterholes. The water motifs and the dancing tracks are more intense and livelier than those used in earlier work at Papunya. The painting implies a much greater area beyond the frame and footprints are used as hieroglyphs for human movement.

Old Mick included several separate creeks and a possum journey among trees looking for bush tucker. His perception of the trees departed from the Aboriginal convention of concentric circles, replacing abstract symbols with compressed bird's-eye distortion. The painting has brilliant strength and is a masterpiece within the painting movement.

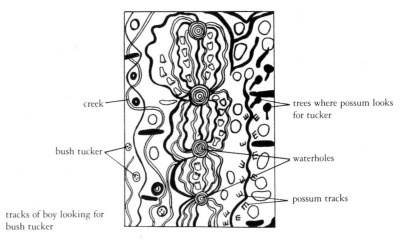

creek
bush tucker
tracks of boy looking for
bush tucker
trees where possum looks
for tucker
waterholes
possum tracks

Bill Stockman Tjapaltjarri (right) and Dinny Nolan Tjampitjinpa at Papunya, 1971.

BILL STOCKMAN TJAPALTJARRI was a proud family man and provided a comfortable humpy for his Pintupi wife and children. On his trips to the big cities he was a wonderful ambassador for his people and always brought home presents for his children. He was one of the busiest of the Papunya painters.

Artist Bill Stockman Tjapaltjarri
Tribe Anmatjira Aranda
Born c 1930
Story Two Quiet Snakes Dreaming
Completed 1972
Size 70 cm long
Location Undetermined
Custodian Tjapaltjarri-Tjungurrayi

This superb carving was made from a large beanwood log about forty centimetres in diameter. Carving and painting took almost two weeks of constant work. There seem to be two different snakes in the carving, resting on a log in the sun. Behind the neck of the first snake are three concentric circles indicating possible sit-down places or fireplaces to do with the Snake Dreaming.

I had asked Bill to do the job 'special well', as it would be a gift to my father. Bill's payment was my transistor radio, which he had wanted to buy for months. It was a good radio and I was in no hurry to be without it, but Bill's special effort seemed to warrant the sacrifice. To my knowledge no Aborigine at the settlement had a radio, and they were highly sought after. Kaapa did the dotting on the tail, as Bill had grown weary of the big job and abandoned it for a painting.

PHOTOGRAPH: ALLAN SCOTT

Johnny Lynch Tjapangati (left), with Tim Leura Tjapaltjarri and Kaapa Tjampitjinpa and son, at Papunya, 1971.

JOHNNY LYNCH TJAPANGATI was a leading stockman at nearby Narwitooma cattle station and was highly regarded in the Aboriginal community for this reason. When dressed as a cowboy, he had a spectacular flamboyance which was quite extraordinary in that settlement. Speaking with an American accent, he told me many adventure stories. Our relationship was slow to develop and Johnny Lynch was the last man to come forward wanting to paint.

Artist Johnny Lynch Tjapangati
Tribe Anmatjira Aranda
Born c 1922 *Died* 1981
Story Honey Ant Dreaming
Completed 1973
Size 59 × 87 cm (ochre & PVA on board)
Location 'Ngawnah' – a long corroboree journey that ends near Woodgreen Station, across the bitumen
Custodian Tjapangati-Tjapananga

This painting is a stylized map of the epic journey of the Honey Ant beings from the west of Australia through Papunya and beyond to the east coast. Papunya is honey ant ground because it was here that the Honey Ant beings had a confrontation with the aggressive Soldier Ant beings. Peace was made without conflict. The straight lines are the honey ants' journey and the concentric circles are the special places in the landscape where they rested. These places later became ceremonial sites. The U signs are the corroboree men telling the story.

Johnny spent a week painting this picture. Originally it was on a background of yellow ochre but, after a discussion with Tim Leura, Johnny over-dotted the yellow with red ochre. The hieroglyph used for the honey ants travelling on each side of the sacred tracks is particularly interesting, as it is the same hieroglyph which Kaapa Tjampitjinpa had agreed to place on the wall of the Papunya school in 1971.

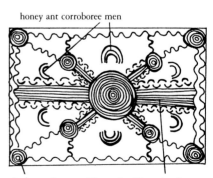

honey ant corroboree men

sit-down place   Honey Ant Dreaming journey

David Corby Tjapaltjarri (right) with Johnny Scobie Tjapangunga at Papunya, 1971.

DAVID CORBY TJAPALTJARRI was Charlie Egalie Tjapaltjarri's brother. A big, heavily built man with a quiet, unassuming manner, he was one of the youngest of all the artists. He had very strong tribal links, despite his background on cattle stations. He painted with less conviction than most of the other artists but was capable and reliable. He left the 'painting mob' to become head stockman on the government cattle station at Haast's Bluff.

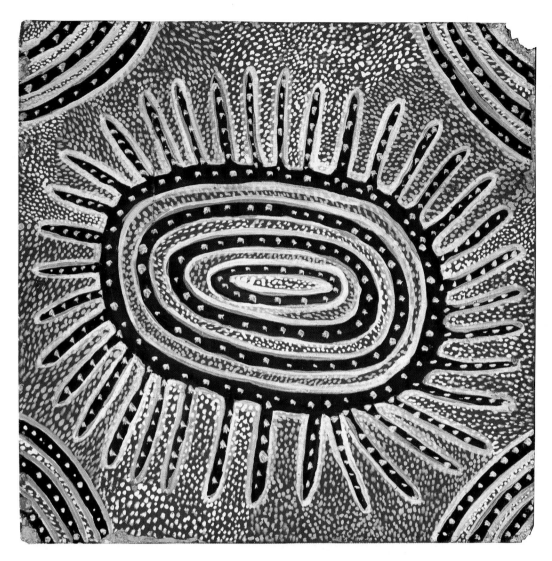

Artist David Corby Tjapaltjarri
Tribe Wailpri
Born c 1940 *Died* 1984
Story Woman's Fire Dreaming
Completed 1973
Size 37 × 37 cm
Location Tjanti, north-west of Vaughan Springs Station
Custodian Tjapaltjarri-Tjungurrayi

A Fire Dreaming celebrates the importance of fire in the lives of the people. It is part of the essence of their way of life. In the old times they would travel with smouldering firesticks and sleep side by side with fires in between. The smoke would keep the flies away and the heat would soothe the body.

Aboriginal people finger the coals with their tough hands and can keep even the tiniest fire under control. Children play a game with the coals, placing them on their skin and attempting to suffer the pain.

In this painting all the women are cooking goannas or kangaroo and have plenty of bush tucker – plums, bananas and raisins. The stylized fireplace is of concentric ovals instead of the more usual concentric circles. The radiating lines are firesticks that the women will whirl above their heads in the ceremony. The sets of arced lines in the four corners are the cliff strata of the particular valley where this ritual takes place. Wailpri art combines the severe simplification of the Pintupi with the symmetrical order of the Anmatjira Aranda.

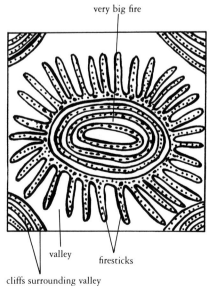

very big fire

valley firesticks

cliffs surrounding valley

CHARLIE TARAWA (TJARURU) TJUNGURRAYI was of medium height and strong build and had worked as a labourer and stockman during his early years. A shrewd man with long experience with Europeans, he was connected with those men who first had come to the art room for assistance. He used vigorous and versatile designs, and had an above-average capacity to explain his paintings. He would call me 'Boss', and always wore a hat to conceal a very severe burn scar on his forehead. He was most responsive to encouragement and the quality of his work rapidly improved. Usually untidy and huskily spoken, he adopted the position of representative of the younger Pintupi group, since Mick Namerari Tjapaltjarri and Old Walter were less articulate. He was somewhat of an adventurer and was always keen to go to town.

One time I was on a short visit to Papunya after a long absence. My gifts of clothing had already gone to painting men of other Pintupi tribes. All I had left were sweets, which I gave to the children because they were not really appropriate for the men. As I was distributing the bags, Charlie came up and roared to the group of Pintupi families, 'That's our boss, that's him.' His attentions made me feel content.

When we were visiting Papunya to make my film *A Calendar of Dreamings*, we needed two Aboriginal actors to walk across the skyline in the manner of traditional hunters, as we had no time to wait for the real thing. Both Charlie and his Pintupi mate Turkey Tolson obliged, with typically firm control and appeal.

As a Pintupi, Charlie lived in a simple grass house and had many wives and children. He was accorded extra prominence by being the eldest of many Tjungurrayi skin brothers. Although he was very amiable I never came to meet any of his family in that obscure society. Charlie had many European experiences, including a trip to England in 1987, but he still lived in the traditional manner.

Artist Charlie Tarawa (Tjaruru) Tjungurrayi
Tribe Pintupi
Born c 1920
Story Ice Dreaming
Completed 1972
Size 60 × 46 cm
Location 'Pinarina', near Lake McKay, in the artist's country west of Sandy Blight Junction, Western Australia
Custodian Tjapaltjarri-Tjungurrayi

This Ice Dreaming describes a site at least four days' walk west of Papunya in very rough country. The concentric circles are ceremonial rock holes. The curved lines on the right-hand side represent cliffs where the people live.

Charlie had received no formal education to make him aware of the scientific nature or geological relevance of ice, but his story has been passed down by word of mouth from the last Ice Age more than thirty thousand years ago. Hail is very common in Central Australia, and Charlie could also speak about ice in the refrigerator and 'when ice made the mountains in my country'.

ceremonial places   country formed by the ice

cliffs

Artist Charlie Tarawa (Tjaruru) Tjungurrayi

Tribe Pintupi

Born c 1920

Story Frog Dreaming

Completed 1973

Size 60 × 46 cm (poster paint & PVA on board)

Location Kalkorintja, a small lake near cliffs in the artist's country, west of Sandy Blight Junction, Western Australia

Custodian Tjapaltjarri-Tjungurrayi

The Frog Dreaming is part of the Ice Dreaming in the custody of the same artist. The tracks of the Frog Spirit Being dominate this painting. Many corroboree men sit around big fires in caves. Outside there is rain, hail and lightning (shown by the spiralling lines and dots).

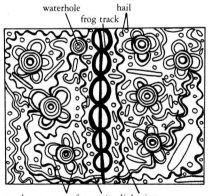

waterhole   hail
frog track

corroboree men at fires   rain   lightning

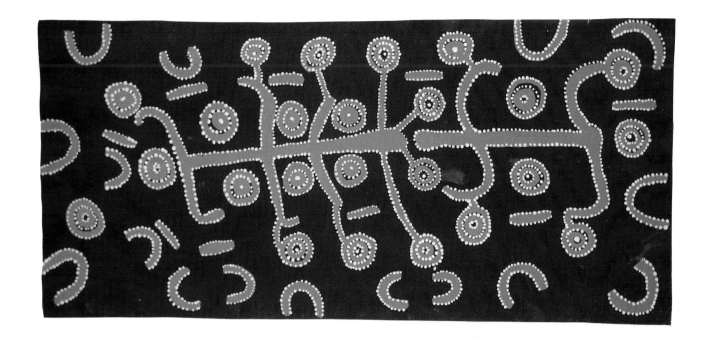

Artist Charlie Tarawa (Tjaruru) Tjungurrayi
Tribe Pintupi
Born c 1920
Story Yam Dreaming
Completed 1972
Size 45 × 75 cm
Location Erawankuna, in the artist's country, west of Sandy Blight Junction, Western Australia
Custodian Tjapaltjarri-Tjungurrayi

The vital, dancing central shapes that represent the yam plants were first painted by Charlie Tarawa on a linoleum floor tile using red paint tinter only. It was most impressive in motif but was of poor physical quality. I asked Charlie to do this Dreaming again, using quality materials and board. He repeated the strange central motif, and completed the story by showing the yam in the ground, its seed and its roots.

Several men are represented by the short, curved lines. Also shown are spears, boomerangs and digging sticks. The painting is for young people, to teach them that the yam plant is a good food, and where and how to find it.

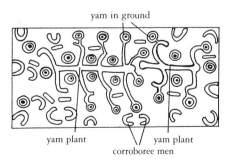

yam in ground

yam plant   yam plant

corroboree men

PHOTOGRAPH: ALLAN SCOTT

Yala Yala Gibbs (right) with Anatjari No. I (left) at Papunya, 1971.

YALA YALA GIBBS TJUNGURRAYI was easily the biggest of the painting men, and he communicated mostly with his hands. His poignant muteness and his size made him conspicuous and disturbing to many people. Yala Yala was one of the first men to visit me at my flat in search of painting materials.

Artist Yala Yala Gibbs Tjungurrayi
Tribe Pintupi
Born c 1930
Story Spider Dreaming
Completed 1971
Size 40 × 80 cm
Location Tjingari, Gibson Desert
Custodian Tjapaltjarri-Tjungurrayi

The central motif is a stylized spider's web joining a set of concentric circles (the sandhill which is its home). The two large oval shapes with linear markings at either end of the web are sandhills. The other sets of concentric circles are fireplaces where corroboree men are sitting down with their boomerangs.

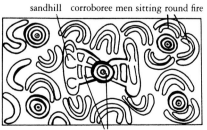

sandhill   corroboree men sitting round fire

ground painting of spider's web and hole

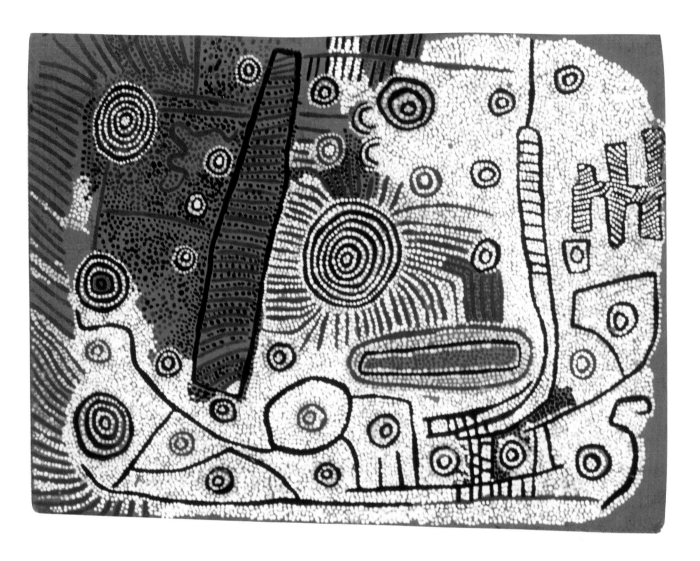

Artist Yala Yala Gibbs Tjungurrayi
Tribe Pintupi
Born c 1930
Story Landscape Dreaming with Trees,
Mountains and Corroboree Journeys
Completed 1972
Size 60 × 40 cm
Location undetermined
Custodian Tjapaltjarri-Tjungurrayi

The motifs used here indicate an epic landscape of unprecedented scale, with vast distances and many features.

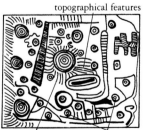

topographical features

vast desert landscape   waterholes

Mick Namerari Tjapaltjarri (left) at Blackwater Outstation with other Pintupi men (left to right: Riley Tjupurrula, Cameron Tjampitjinpa, Turkey Tolson Tjupurrula and Johnny Scobie Tjapangunga).

MICK NAMERARI TJAPALTJARRI was a man of slight and purposeful conversation. His material possessions consisted of a twelve-gauge double-barrel shotgun and a tape recorder. He worked with single-mindedness and lived by himself, happily, it seemed, in a transitional house.

Mick was very comfortable as the star of my film *Mick and the Moon* (1979). The story told of how an Aboriginal man believed he owned the moon, and how his duty was to paint ceremonial pictures to fulfil this belief. Many beautiful visual effects were achieved in the film, which was screened around the world.

In Sydney, when we were making the film, I took Mick and Tim Leura to a screening of *Rocky*, the boxing movie. I had assumed both Aboriginal men would like this programme, but it made them very sad and they hated it. 'Too much hurt,' they said.

Artist Mick Namerari Tjapaltjarri
Tribe Pintupi
Born c 1925
Story Family Moon Dreaming
Completed 1976
Size 50 × 40 cm
Location West-south-west of Papunya
Custodian Tjapaltjarri-Tjungurrayi

This painting was one of a series of six painted for my film, *Mick and the Moon*. It is extraordinarily powerful. It was painted at my parents' home in Randwick, Sydney, where part of the film was made. It is not a detailed story, but only one aspect of the story of the moon, and is valuable for what it shows of Aboriginal cosmology.

Four people are shown sitting around a central sand mosaic of the moon, which is depicted in very warm yellow and red ochre. They are singing in happiness for the summer full moon, when it is usual for people to sit up all night, turning night into day.

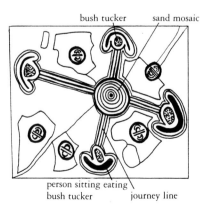

bush tucker   sand mosaic

person sitting eating
bush tucker   journey line

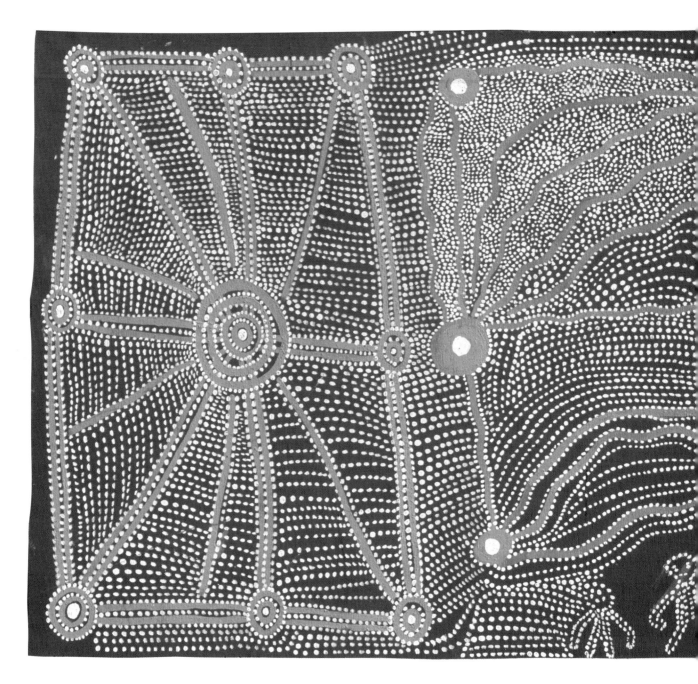

Artist Mick Namerari Tjapaltjarri
Tribe Pintupi
Born c 1925
Story Naughty Boys' Dreaming
Completed 1971
Size 42 × 65 cm
Location Marlpi, west of Sandy Blight
Junction, Western Australia
Custodian Tjapaltjarri-Tjungurrayi (Mick
says this story belongs to everyone: all people
and all tribes.)

The story of naughty boys being punished is
used by many of the artists. This simple,
brilliant story uses lines and dots and only
two colors. Some naughty boys have taken
many sap lollies from mulga trees that sur-
round a large waterhole (indicated by concentric circles) a long way south-west of
Papunya, in sandhill country. The top of the
painting contains a stylized map of the
waterhole, the surrounding mulga trees and
the many paths made by people walking to

and from the waterhole. Two old men are
indicated by arms and trunk only. Their
boomerangs are included bottom left. The
bottom section of the painting represents the
land surface. The circles here are trees, perhaps desert oak, and the weaving, curved
lines are the form of the sandhills. The
dotting in this area represents the sand and
vegetation, and the short, hatched lines represent grass.

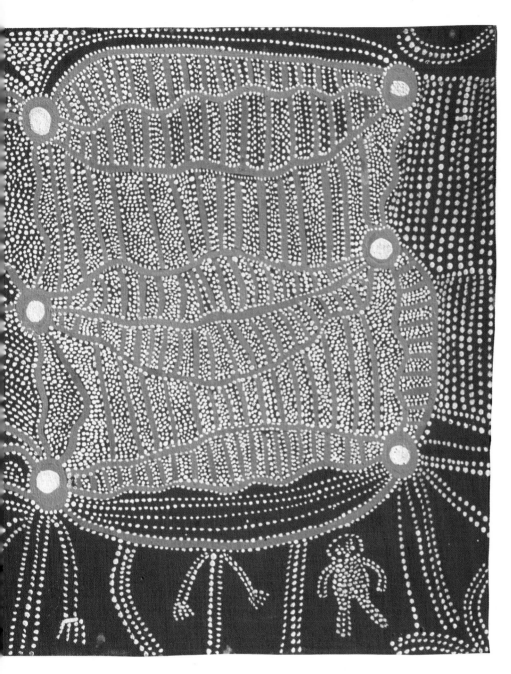

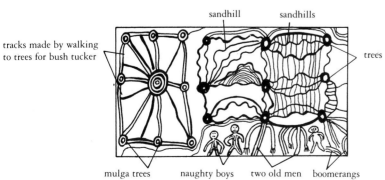

tracks made by walking
to trees for bush tucker

sandhill   sandhills

trees

mulga trees   naughty boys   two old men   boomerangs

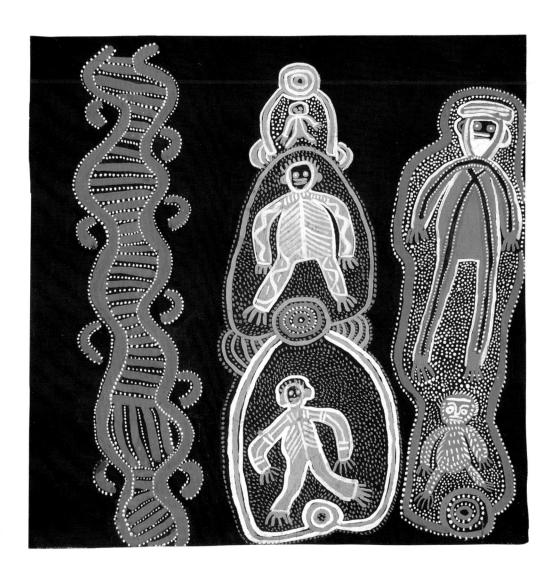

Artist Mick Namerari Tjapaltjarri
Tribe Pintupi
Born c 1925
Story Family Bush Tucker Dreaming
Completed 1972
Size 48 × 48 cm (poster paint & PVA on board)
Location Marlpi, west of Sandy Blight Junction, Western Australia
Custodian Tjapaltjarri-Tjungurrayi

This painting is a fine example of the absence of perspective in Pintupi art and the reduc-tion of all objects to a flat design. The multiple situations give the painting a strong narrative quality.

This story is one of domestic happiness. In accordance with Aboriginal custom, each member of the family has their own fire. They are warm in the night's coolness, sit-ting inside windbreaks and eating bush raisins, yams and witchetty grubs. The body paint indicates that they are celebrating a bush tucker ritual. The spiralling band and pattern represent the earth where the grubs are found. The grubs are shown by simple curves.

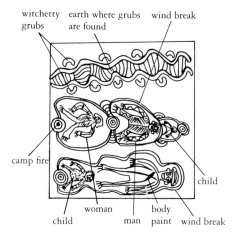

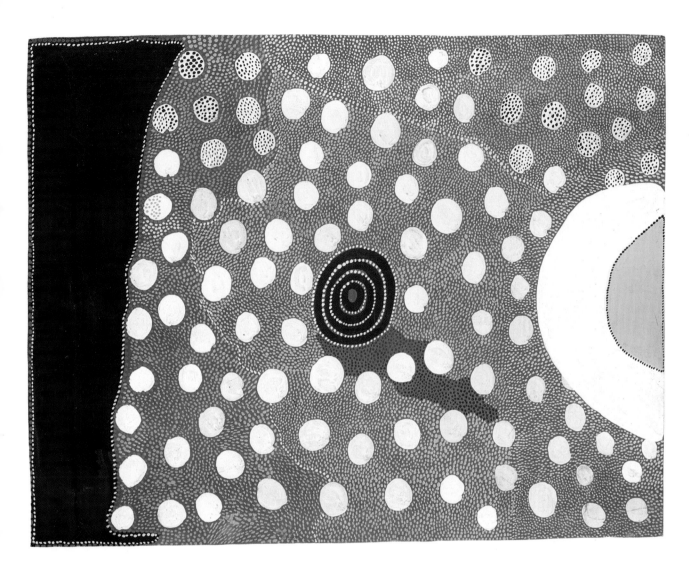

Artist Mick Namerari Tjapaltjarri
Tribe Pintupi
Born c 1925
Story Rising Sun Chasing the Night Away
Dreaming
Completed 1978
Size 40 × 60 cm
Location Western Australia
Custodian Tjapaltjarri-Tjungurrayi

This outstanding depiction of the night and its phases was specially painted for my film *Mick and the Moon*. It is startling in its visualization of the sun upon the landscape. The point of view seems to be from within the heavens, looking down through the stars, past the sun rising on the right of the painting and the night on the left, and onto the campfires burning on the great night plain beneath. The painting is a powerful testimony to the Aboriginal sense of perspective.

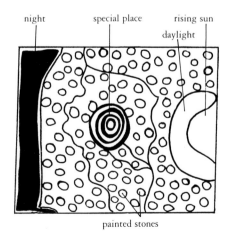

night   special place   rising sun
daylight

painted stones

89

PHOTOGRAPH: JON FALKENMIRE

CHARLIE EGALIE TJAPALTJARRI was a powerfully built man in his early forties who had spent most of his life as a stockman, principally on the Haast's Bluff and Narwitooma stations, where he proved extremely reliable. He was David Corby's brother and was married with several children. He had custody of the Wallaby Dreaming, the Sugar Ant Dreaming and many bush tucker stories.

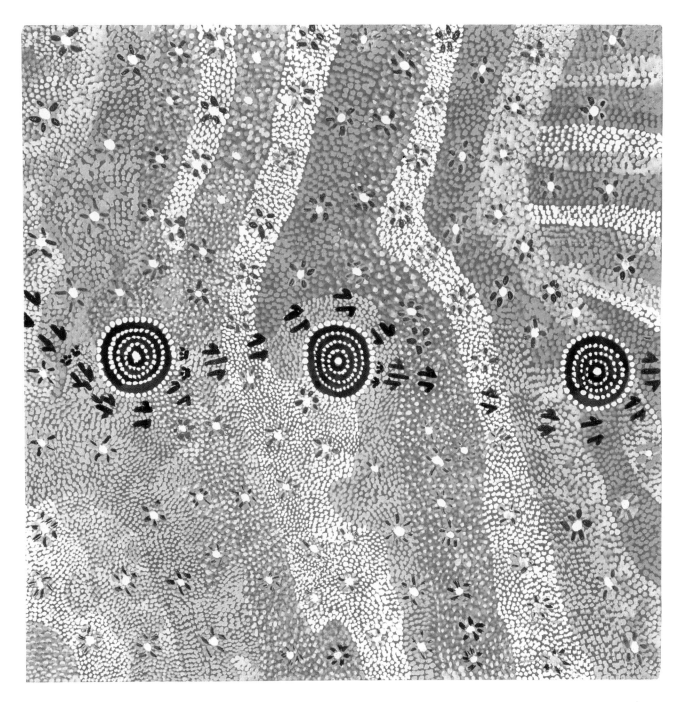

Artist Charlie Egalie Tjapaltjarri
Tribe Wailpri
Born c 1938
Story Wallaby Dreaming in the Sandhills
Completed 1977
Size 50 × 50 cm
Location North-west of Papunya, near
Yuendumu
Custodian Tjapaltjarri-Tjungurrayi

A Wallaby Spirit Being is making a journey
across sandhill country east of Yuendumu.
His path is shown by the tracks as he moves
from one waterhole (concentric circles) to
another. The sandhills are indicated by bands
of dotting across the painting. All kinds of
bush tucker, grass and sand are shown in
between.

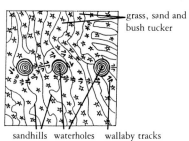

grass, sand and
bush tucker

sandhills waterholes wallaby tracks

John Tjakamarra at Papunya, 1971.

J OHN TJAKAMARRA This quiet man was difficult to understand, apparently even among his own Pintupi people. His wispy beard and gentle manner gave him an unchanging ascetic aura. He often painted undistinguished designs and seemed unable to produce the variety that I encouraged.

Artist John Tjakamarra
Tribe Pintupi
Born c 1940
Story Kangaroo and Wallaby Joke Story
Completed 1971
Size 40 × 80 cm
Location Tjingari, Gibson Desert
Custodian Tjakamarra-Tjupurrula

The concentric circles at the centre of this design represent a waterhole. The U-shaped loops are the corroboree men. The tracks and tail marks of the wallaby cross the painting in both directions. Meanwhile a large kangaroo has travelled quickly across the same area from top to bottom.

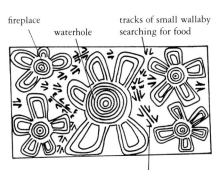

fireplace
waterhole
tracks of small wallaby searching for food
tracks of big kangaroo going south

93

Artist John Tjakamarra
Tribe Pintupi
Born c 1940
Story Man's Corroboree
Completed 1971
Size 40 × 90 cm
Location Tjingari, Gibson Desert
Custodian Tjakamarra-Tjupurrula

This design is a forthright attempt to imitate traditional sand mosaic art. It is an early work painted on my verandah, and its simplicity gives the design its considerable strength.

All the concentric circles linked by a linear maze represent a sand painting at the corroboree site. The U shapes are the corroboree men seated for the ritual according to their rank and authority. The ceremony is a hunting and bush tucker occasion in which the men thank the Dreaming Spirit forces and invoke their help.

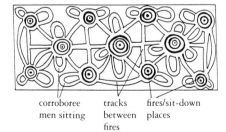

corroboree   tracks   fires/sit-down
men sitting   between   places
               fires

PHOTOGRAPH: ALLAN SCOTT

UTA UTA TJANGALA was a most obscure Pintupi man. I first knew him when he was the gardener hosing lawns in the park near my flat. He showed great vigour in his early drawings and went on to produce marvellous work of great importance to Aboriginal culture. Uta Uta was humble and eccentric, with an explosive laugh, a struggling, pained expression and bizarre clothes. He often carried boomerangs in his belt. Uta Uta was devoted to his wife, Gnalia, who was crippled and whom he moved around in a wheelbarrow.

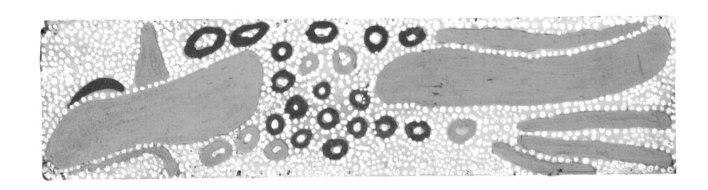

Artist Uta Uta Tjangala
Tribe Pintupi
Born c 1935
Story Man's Bush Tucker Dreaming
Completed 1971
Size 15 × 45 cm (poster paint & PVA on board)
Location West of Sandy Blight Junction, Western Australia
Custodian Tjangala-Tjampitjinpa

A man is looking for bush tucker in the sandhills and his footprints and finger marks are shown in the sand. He is searching for witchetty grubs in the holes shown by hollow circles. This is a very 'quiet' story, in that it involves nothing secret-sacred, either explicitly or implicitly.

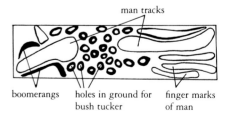

man tracks

boomerangs   holes in ground for   finger marks
               bush tucker   of man

96

Artist Uta Uta Tjangala
Tribe Pintupi
Born c 1935
Story Boys' Corroboree Dreaming
Completed 1972
Size 45 × 58 cm
Location West of Sandy Blight Junction, Western Australia
Custodian Tjangala-Tjampitjinpa

Three boys sit at a fireplace beside a large sand mosaic where there are boys' tjurungas laid on the sand. The boys are wearing body decoration. The ground painting is quite elaborate, the series of straight lines that meet the central concentric circles denoting that Dreaming journeys cross at this site. The straight lines denote travelling and the circles sit-down places.

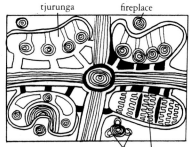

Artist Uta Uta Tjangala
Tribe Pintupi
Born c 1935
Story Snake Dreaming
Completed 1972
Size 45 × 58 cm
Location West of Sandy Blight Junction,
Western Australia
Custodian Tjangala-Tjampitjinpa

The Snake Dreaming is a widely distributed
story which is especially important in Pintupi culture. It is believed that the Snake
Dreaming men came from the south, cross-
ing many tribal areas, including Uluru, Lake
Macdonald and Haast's Bluff, passing west of

Papunya into Pintupi country, then into
Wailpri country to a major ceremonial site
for this snake totem at Hooker Creek. They
made waterholes, creeks and surface features.
Decorative motifs in paintings can be the
scales of a snake, its meat and its skeleton. In
this painting for children the short, curved
shapes are two boys sitting beside a ground
drawing for a Snake Dreaming. One boy has
a fire. A snake is drawn bottom left in a
similar shape to that of the sand mosaic.
A big cave is indicated by the dark curve
bottom right, which is the site where this
ceremony takes place. Top right a dark,
scalloped curve indicates a waterhole with
running water. Somewhat softer in color than

Uta Uta's usually severe work, the painting
is divided into four sections balanced around
a central pivotal point.

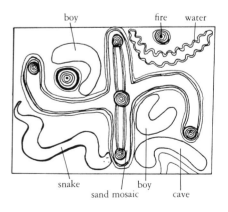

Shorty Lungkata Tjungurrayi with his daughter in 1971.

SHORTY LUNGKATA TJUNGURRAYI was a stocky, nimble man who was an expert hunter, a wonderful dancer and a leader in the Pintupi community. I never knew him to use any English at all. His deep, resonant voice would breathe 'Yawow' (Very good) and he would nod in dignified agreement with anything I asked him. Other Pintupi or Johnny Warrangkula would assist by translating. Shorty would look at me when I spoke but would always answer to the other men or talk to his painting. He never asked me for anything and was impervious to any disturbance. His work was singularly intense, with its own powerful truth.

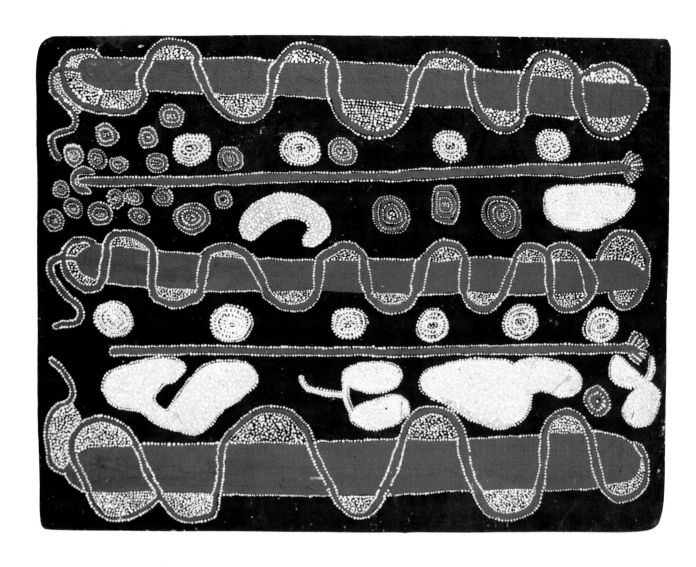

Artist Shorty Lungkata Tjungurrayi
Tribe Pintupi
Born c 1920 *Died* 1987
Story Bush Banana Dreaming
Completed 1972
Size 45 × 60 cm
Location Tjingari, Gibson Desert
Custodian Tjapaltjarri-Tjungurrayi

This painting is in the Papunya school collection. The three thick vertical shapes are the trees where the bush banana grows. The two thin vertical shapes are women's digging sticks. The simple white shapes are the bush bananas. The concentric circles are fireplaces for the bush banana corroboree. The spiralling line that seems to entwine the trees is ceremonial hair string for the corroboree. The cluster of small concentric circles at the top left of the painting is a group of women and children.

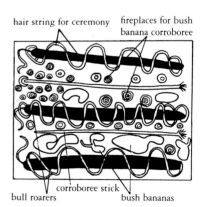

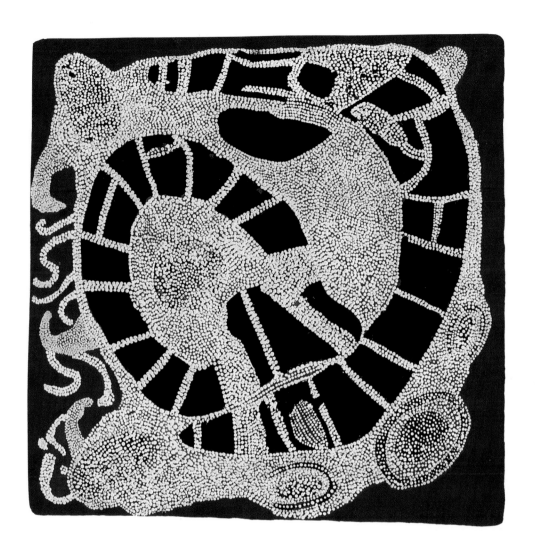

Artist Shorty Lungkata Tjungurrayi
Tribe Pintupi
Born c 1920 *Died* 1987
Story Snake Dreaming
Completed 1972
Size 35 × 35 cm
Location Tjingari, Gibson Desert
Custodian Tjapaltjarri-Tjungurrayi

Two quiet snakes are resting in the sun and lying on the sand. Earlier, two Aboriginal hunters had been digging in the ground for the snakes but they got away. The banded, curved black shapes are the snakes. The dotted black circle in the middle of the painting is a small cave. Two snake men at fireplaces are shown by the U shapes. The hole in which the snakes live is shown between the two snake corroboree men who are performing this ritual.

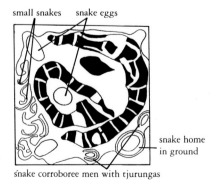

small snakes   snake eggs

snake home
in ground

snake corroboree men with tjurungas

PHOTOGRAPH: ALLAN SCOTT

A NATJARI NO. III TJAKAMARRA was a most accomplished painter who painted many Pintupi Dreamings about his special homeland, Kiwirrkura. He had little experience with Europeans and was a quiet man who spoke in whispers.

Artist Anatjari No. III Tjakamarra
Tribe Pintupi
Born c 1938
Story Homeland Snake Dreaming
Completed 1975
Size 60 × 80 cm
Location Artist's country, south-west of
Sandy Blight Junction, Western Australia
Custodian Tjakamarra-Tjupurrula

The simple curved line surrounding the set of
concentric circles represents a lake and a
claypan where women have speared a snake.
They cook and eat the snake. The curved line
is a stylized simplification of an actual place,
'Kulamuku', in Anatjari's homeland region.
Women are central to this Dreaming ceremony
but men and young people are also involved.

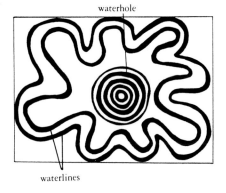

TIM PAYUNGKA TJAPANGATI would visit me at my quarters with all the other Pintupi men who had just finished work at the farm. Tim's boyish enthusiasm and happy confidence made him the most productive of the Pintupi, and he created startling images from the beginning. It was not uncommon for a Pintupi artist to paint one picture, only to erase it and quickly paint another, and Tim was no exception.

One time there was fighting in the camp and Tim suffered a punctured lung. Tim was a classic Aboriginal warrior and his physical condition, like that of so many Pintupi people, deteriorated rapidly with white fellow food.

Tim Payungka would work with bold confidence on his paintings, and his exuberant laughter reminded me of many uninhibited friends of past years. I felt comfortable with him as he taught and corrected me in my efforts to learn Pidgin/Pintupi, always regaled with laughter.

Artist Tim Payungka Tjapangati
Tribe Pintupi
Born c 1938
Story Goanna and Dingo Dreaming
Completed 1973
Size 60 × 50 cm
Location Tjingari, Gibson Desert
Custodian Tjapangati-Tjapananga

This painting is in the Papunya school collection. Tim painted it after the wonderful reception received by an earlier painting of his, 'Children's Possum Dreaming' (See page 107), which I asked him to copy. The telling of any story in the form of a painting was quite subjective and dependant on physical touch and feeling; it was therefore impossible to reproduce the work. This adventure story is apparently being told by the corroboree man shown at the bottom of the painting in elaborate attire. He is holding a boomerang and pointing to the giant goanna, which seems to float in space with the corroboree man and the two dingoes in a menacing attack. The lovely patterns on all of these figures are complemented by the clustered dotting pattern of the goanna bush tucker that comprises the background.

possum attacking goanna   bush tucker for goanna

goanna

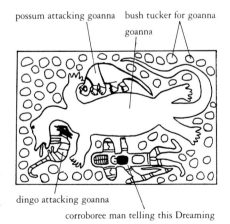

dingo attacking goanna

corroboree man telling this Dreaming

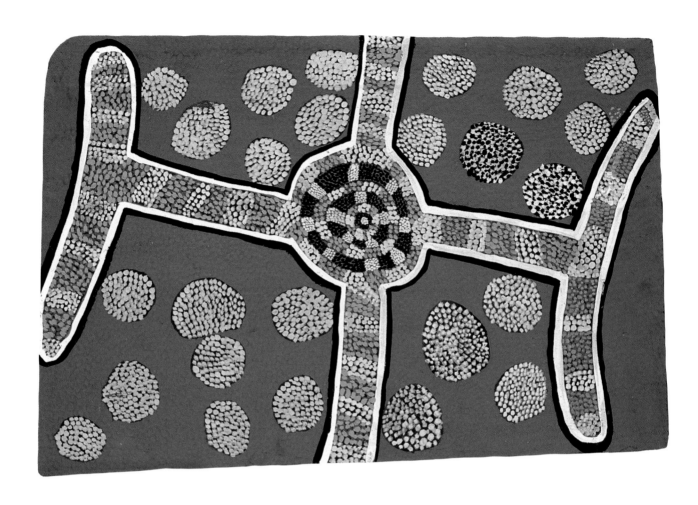

Artist Tim Payungka Tjapangati
Tribe Pintupi
Born c 1938
Story Milky Way Dreaming
Completed 1971
Size 54 × 35 cm (poster paint & PVA on board)
Location Tjingari, Gibson Desert
Custodian Tjapangati-Tjapananga

Tim Payungka says all tribes have this story but they give quite different tellings of it. One account explains how seven sisters whose husband was murdered poisoned the murderer and flew away on a corroboree pole to become the Milky Way in the sky. The painting reveals marvellous simplification of observed celestial objects. The powerful patterned shape in the centre is the constellation of stars across the sky.

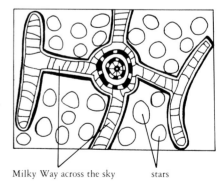

Milky Way across the sky   stars

Artist Tim Payungka Tjapangati
Tribe Pintupi
Born c 1938
Story Children's Possum Dreaming
Completed 1972
Size 60 × 50 cm
Location Tjingari, Gibson Desert
Custodian Tjapangati-Tjapananga

This painting came about when the painting men were preparing children's stories for public exhibition in Alice Springs but it was later stolen and has not been traced. Two boys wearing body paint are sitting at a fireplace, holding hands. Either the fire is very big or the boys are very small. The zig-zagging white lines represent a ground painting, as do the short oblique white lines, which are repeated on the boys' arms. The possum's track is shown in the sand. According to Aboriginal tradition, the Possum Spirit Being is curious, kind and active.

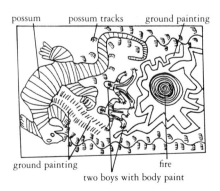

possum   possum tracks   ground painting

ground painting   fire

two boys with body paint

Kaapa Tjampitjinpa and his two sons at Papunya, 1972.

KAAPA TJAMPITJINPA was painting before I arrived at Papunya. He used scrap wood, fibro cement sheets and school slates, and had been dismissed as a school yardman for allegedly stealing brushes. The painting movement was built around this man's compulsive will and extraordinary ability to paint. Kaapa's spatial control, elegant symmetry, classic balance and exquisite filigree variations on decorative motifs gave his work its distinctive monumental presence and heraldic clarity and splendour.

However, the social tensions within the painting group spilled over ferociously into his work. He was the most vigorously symmetrical of the painters, yet his paintings are a compendium of sacred signs with secular subject matter. Kaapa consistently allowed the secular and sacred to clash in his symbology. His intrusive icons were forever commenting on (and thereby, it seemed to me, questioning) the tribal traditions. Along with sacredness and secrecy, Kaapa threw his traditions to the winds, expressing instead a grim horror of the environment he was obliged to endure in the here-and-now.

Artist Kaapa Tjampitjinpa
Tribe Anmatjira Aranda
Born c 1928 *Died* 1990
Story Wild Orange Dreaming
Completed 1971
Size 45 × 60 cm (ochre & PVA on board)
Location Undetermined
Custodian Tjangala-Tjampitjinpa

This skilfully painted version of the Wild
Orange Dreaming shows traditional symmetry as well as European influences.

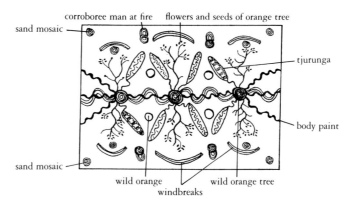

Artist Kaapa Tjampitjinpa
Tribe Anmatjira Aranda
Born c 1928 *Died* 1990
Story Rainbow Storm Dreaming
Completed 1971
Size 30 × 45 cm (poster paint & PVA on board)
Location Mikanji, a rain-making site near Mount Denison in the Western Desert of Central Australia
Custodian Tjangala-Tjampitjinpa

This painting is an interesting formalization of the component elements of the Water Dreaming: water men in caves, rain, clouds, rainbow, running water, waterholes and underground water. Kaapa persistently integrated body decoration motifs of the corroboree man into his paintings on hardboard.

The spiralling lines represent falling rain. The two U shapes are the Water Dreaming corroboree men sitting at the Dreaming site, Mikanji, which is shown by the large concentric ovals with radiating lines. The other ovals and concentric circles represent waterholes and are associated with both sand painting and body decoration. The intensive overall patterning and spirals show the heavy rain that splashes onto the sand and flows across the land surface into rivers that will run further into the desert, to soak underground. The two water corroboree men have power and custody of these rock holes and underground water that is found by digging. The dark spiralling line across the centre of the painting is the rainbow after the storm.

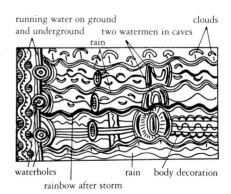

running water on ground and underground — clouds
two watermen in caves
rain
waterholes — rainbow after storm — rain — body decoration

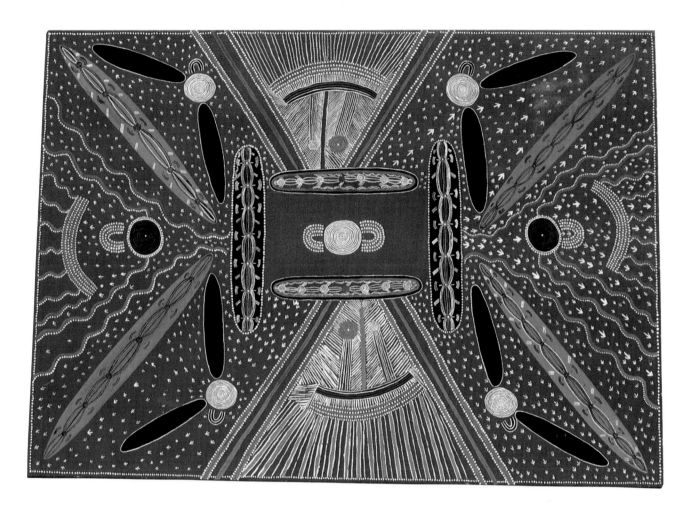

Artist Kaapa Tjampitjinpa
Tribe Anmatjira Aranda
Born c 1928 *Died* 1990
Story Budgerigar Dreaming
Completed 1972
Size 70 × 45 cm
Location South-west Yuendumu
Custodian Tjangala-Tjampitjinpa

The budgerigar corroboree is a major teaching occasion. The ceremonies involve stages of advancement towards the manhood initiation occasion itself. The painting of this budgerigar ritual stage can be seen by all persons. This story concerns young people sitting in the learning area for instruction.

There are many different versions of the ceremony. The teacher men are identified with budgerigars. The grass seed for them is called 'Wanganu'. The new growth after rain brings vast numbers of these 'little green birds'.

This painting features radiating tjurungas marked with totemic budgerigar signs, symbols for fireplaces, a ground mosaic Dreaming and the symbol for a man in a ceremonial grouping. Bird tracks radiate from a dominant centre circle. Body paint patterns are consciously decorative yet sensitively restrained as they intuitively link the oval shapes. The classic order of the painting is evidence of advanced design reasoning. Such

visual boldness depends to a certain extent on modern painting methods and the use of brushes and paint, surpassing the severe limitations of traditional techniques.

body decoration for corroboree

corroboree man at fire

young boys for corroboree

tjurungas for budgerigar corroboree

CLIFFORD POSSUM TJAPALTJARRI   Clifford was lithe and strongly
built but not as tall as Tim Leura. In conversation he was brief and he had
a fine sense of decorum. He needed nothing explained to him. What
Clifford had done before working with the painters, I do not know. He had been
a stockman at Napperby, but then apparently became unemployed. This
situation was common. Most of the work available on the settlement was menial
and made little sense to the Aborigines.

Clifford worked very hard on his complex of designs. His technique with the
brush was intricate and he seemed interested in three-dimensional illusion and
realism, which made his work quite European. Modulated tone and broken color
produced a fractured series of shapes with extraordinary visual effect. His
precision was typical of all the Anmatjira Aranda, and he used colors to achieve a
'shot' effect – blending orange into red, yellow into orange – by means of
stippling. In some of his stories Clifford attempted to give a visual impression of
sunlight, cloud, shadow, earth, to denote specific times of day. His feeling for
form did not depend on outline or drawing but was illusionistic, whereby the
forms merged into one another or into the tone of the background. This
approach seemed to develop over a period of time, especially when so much
special attention was shown towards the work of Johnny Warrangkula, which
also tended towards a kind of tremulous illusion.

In the later stages of the painting movement, Clifford did not really apply
himself, yet his early work was all wonderful. His first painting, an Emu
Dreaming with a realistic corroboree man dancing as the centre piece, was quite
spectacular. The painting showed superlative skill and some European influences
in the realism of the man and the emus. (It is not included here as it contains
some secret-sacred material.)

Artist Clifford Possum Tjapaltjarri
Tribe Anmatjira Aranda
Born c 1940
Story Honey Ant Dreaming
Completed 1972
Size 43 × 58 cm
Location Long way east of Yuendumu into the sunrise
Custodian Tjapaltjarri-Tjungurrayi

The honey ant still does what the ancestor beings did in the Dreamtime: it comes out of the ground, makes a journey and returns to the ground. As indicated by the straight lines through the centre of this design, the Honey Ant beings are travelling east through Yuendumu. The concentric circles are sit-down places during this Dreaming journey. The radiating curved lines are the tracks of the honey ant men going about looking for the honey bag. The nebulous yellow shapes are the honey bags and the white areas with red background are the land. Intense dotting unifies the patchy effect caused by irregular shapes and gives the painting an impressive decorative splendour.

sit-down places   Dreaming journey

honey bags   honey ant men looking for honey

Artist Clifford Possum Tjapaltjarri
Tribe Anmatjira Aranda
Born c 1940
Story Man's Love Story
Completed 1973
Size 43 × 58 cm
Location Napperby Station
Custodian Tjapaltjarri-Tjungurrayi

An old man is singing to entice a woman to join him. (The older a man is, the more power he has with his tongue and the greater his tribal authority. He can even sing a law breaker to death.) He will use a string to secure her and bring her to him. Tracks indicate where he is looking around for her. The circular motifs are body paint for a corroboree. One of the extraordinary qualities of the Western Desert paintings is that they are a visual writing and speak to an Aborigine as assuredly as any European scripts do to Europeans. For any Western Desert Aborigine, the location of this story is immediately identifiable by its hieroglyphs as Napperby Station.

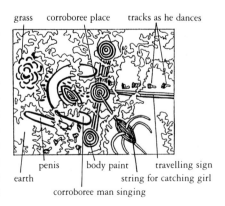

grass   corroboree place   tracks as he dances

penis   body paint   travelling sign
earth   string for catching girl
corroboree man singing

Artist Clifford Possum Tjapaltjarri
Tribe Anmatjira Aranda
Born c 1940
Story Sun Dreaming
Completed 1972
Size 43 × 58 cm
Location Arrangeh, east of Mount Allan and north of Papunya
Custodian Tjapaltjarri-Tjungurrayi

This painting describes the passion of physical love whereby an old man captures the girl of his song. Here, Clifford paints in exultation and happiness, using the incandescence of the sun as a metaphor for love. The painting gives a visual image of sunlight, cloud, shadow and the earth. It is a variant of 'Man's Love Story' (See page 115).

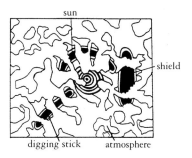

Tim Leura Tjapaltjarri and family at Papunya in 1972. Tim's wife, Daisy, is absent.

TIM LEURA TJAPALTJARRI   Tim's style was much softer than that of the other painters. He was a relatively ordered, systematic painter. His clarity of arrangement gave his work marvellous spatial strength. Yet, beyond an apparently bland symmetry, he used the masking device of implying many shapes in the same hieroglyph, or allowing the hieroglyph to run into another shape, as in the figures in 'Yam Spirit Dreaming' (See page 120) and 'Marriage Dreaming' (See page 124). He was ambiguous in his use of figures and he often used color to diminish outlines between parts of his painting.

Tim had a great feeling for the Yam Dreaming and the Butterfly Dreaming and did not care much for depictions of hunting activities. Later (in 1980) he painted, with some assistance from Clifford Possum, a Death Spirit Dreaming about seven metres in length. It was not a happy painting. It was a savagely brooding, terse journey, with the black human death emblem watching over the enormous, sinuous story track. It was extraordinarily autobiographical.

Through the work of Tim Leura, perhaps, the Western Desert tradition had ceased to be merely a visual, haptic category of communal painting and had become instead at least one man's way of understanding himself as separate from all others. Perhaps I was seeing in his painting the end of a tradition of more than thirty thousand years.

Tim Leura became very ill, distressed by European hegemony. He stumbled about the camps and Alice Springs, a broken and disappointed man. He often used to ring me from Alice Springs. But then I was ill also, and I could not help any more. So, in spite of everything, and to my eternal disappointment, I did not go back to the desert to help Tim. I was unable to return for a long time and could do nothing. Tim Leura died very badly.

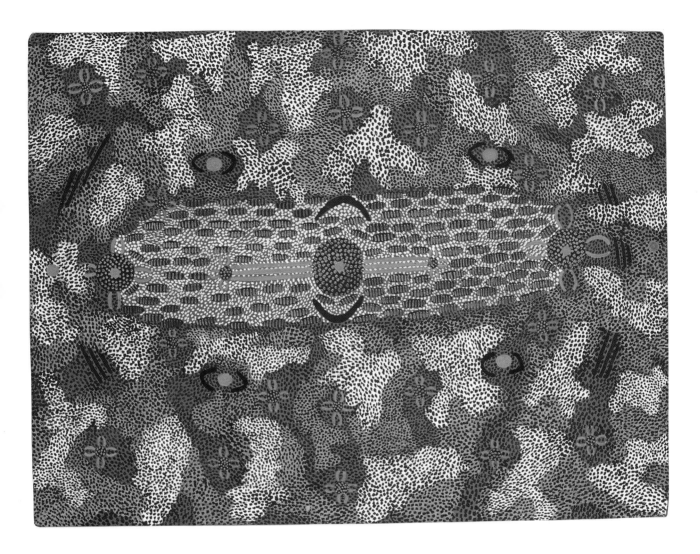

Artist Tim Leura Tjapaltjarri
Tribe Anmatjira Aranda
Born c 1936 *Died* 1984
Story Butterfly Dreaming
Completed 1972
Size 35 × 45 cm
Location Napperby Station
Custodian Tjapaltjarri-Tjungurrayi

This Dreaming concerns the blue butterfly that lives in the mulga scrubland after rain. The central tjurunga form is a sand painting of the butterfly eggs in the nest. Two butterfly corroboree men are sitting across a fireplace shown by the concentric circles. The U shape indicates the men. The butterfly responds to the fresh atmosphere after rain and the new growth of flowers, for the rain has made the earth new again. The small dots represent the sand where a new camp has been made. The dotted areas represent white grass, but not spinifex grass. Tim painted this design during an exhibition in a Sydney department store. Watercolors by his companion, Keith Namatjira (Aranda), were selling well and Tim was very aware of the relative unpopularity of his traditional work. One of the shop assistants was friendly towards Tim, and out of gratitude for her interest Tim painted her a present when he left. It was a painting similar to this one.

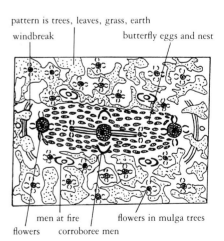

pattern is trees, leaves, grass, earth

windbreak

butterfly eggs and nest

men at fire

flowers

corroboree men

flowers in mulga trees

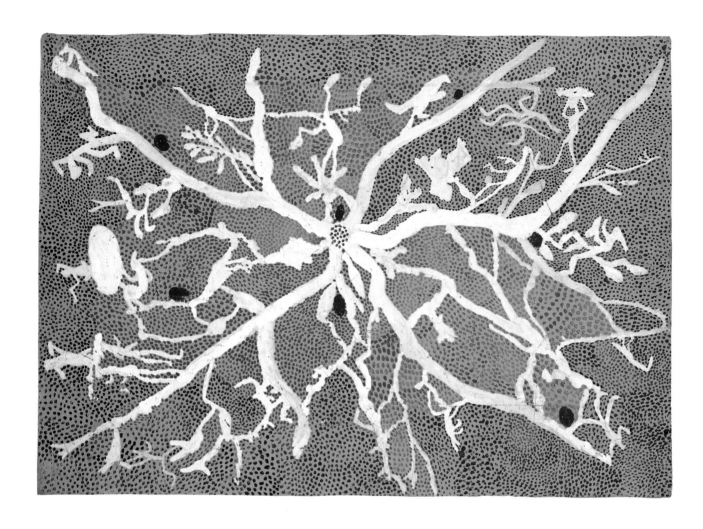

Artist Tim Leura Tjapaltjarri
Tribe Anmatjira Aranda
Born c 1936 *Died* 1984
Story Yam Spirit Dreaming
Completed 1972
Size 54 × 70 cm (poster paint & PVA on board)
Location North-west of Napperby Station
Custodian The artist's father, Barney Turner Tjungurrayi

This definitive painting shows many human figures seeming to emerge from the roots of the yam and doing their various work. The artist has depicted the figures in the same white ochre color as the plant, implying that they have the same spiritual substance as what they are seeking: the yam. It is as though the story proponents become what they do. The areas of light stippling are grass. Dark stippling shows where grass has been burnt away in search of the yam.

This painting has a masterly control of its subject matter and shows great insight into Aboriginal truth. It is quite outside the range of the other Aboriginal artists and, I believe, represents the most important of Tim Leura's paintings.

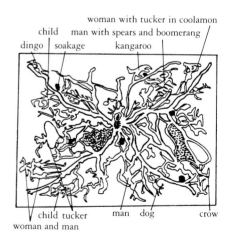

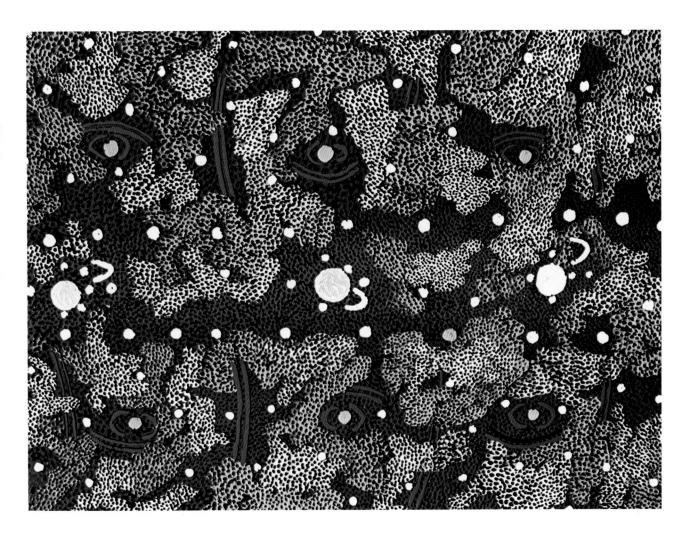

Artist Tim Leura Tjapaltjarri
Tribe Anmatjira Aranda
Born c 1936 *Died* 1984
Story Sun, Moon and Morning Star
Dreaming
Completed 1973
Size 45 × 58 cm (poster paint & PVA on
board)
Location Kerila, near Iluma
Custodian Tjapaltjarri-Tjungurrayi

In Aboriginal tradition the sun represents a man and the moon is a woman. Here, corroboree men sit behind windbreaks with their fires. The fragmented shapes are the clouds and the atmosphere at night. This is a love story and the movement of the sun and the moon across the sky is part of their continuing love adventure. The stars are the campfires of long-ago warriors who have now flown into the sky. The Morning Star, or Daylight Star, is particularly important to the dancers as they wait for daylight.

clouds and
atmosphere at night

all the stars in the sky

stars

moon

sun | windbreaks | sun

moon

corroboree men sitting at fire

Artist Tim Leura Tjapaltjarri, assisted by
Clifford Possum Tjapaltjarri
Tribe Anmatjira Aranda
Born c 1936 *Died* 1984
Story Napperby Death Spirit Dreaming
Completed 1980
Size 213 × 701 cm (acrylic on canvas)
Location Napperby Station
Custodian Tjapaltjarri-Tjungurrayi

This enormous painting, of which the Dreaming map on pages 4–5 is the spiritual outline, is an extraordinary history of Tim Leura's life. It contains huge 'windows' or emblems depicting his life's Dreamings – the Yam Spirit Dreaming, Old Man's Dreaming, Sun and Moon Dreaming – linked by the classic journey line running from east to west across the painting. The death figure in the journey reflects Tim's growing pessimism toward the end of his life. The painting was completed specially for a film I had intended to make in 1980 about Tim's life called *The*

Difference between Photographs. It is revolutionary in the context of Western Desert art because, through it, Tim appeared to be stepping outside his immediate tribal affiliations to comment on the various aspects of spirituality in his own life. He thus turned ostensibly Aboriginal icons into personal and deeply felt representations of his soul's journey. This painting is also an encyclopedic representation of Tim's Aboriginal values, a masterly statement of a life dismayed by the brutality and indifference of the Europeans to what Tim believed were his own lands.

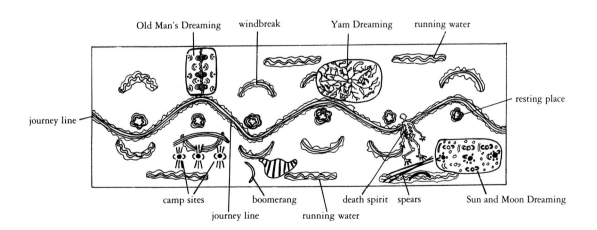

Artist Tim Leura Tjapaltjarri
Tribe Anmatjira Aranda
Born c 1936 *Died* 1984
Story Marriage Dreaming, Tjungurrayi-Nungala
Completed 1978, Sydney
Size 60 × 46 cm
Location North-north-west of the Macdonnell Ranges, possibly Napperby Station at Marembiah
Custodian Tjapaltjarri-Tjungurrayi

Tim did this painting as a gift for me on the occasion of my wedding. As a Tjungurrayi I was Tim Leura's son, which is how he often considered me. The correct skin partner for a Tjungurrayi is a Nungala. The boundaries of the painting indicate a very lengthy journey with many sit-down places. The marriage couple are in the centre of the painting over a fireplace. At either end, the families of the couple sing for the happiness of the marriage. The painting has great richness and subtlety of coloring but the principle figures are concealed, an early instance of the systematic suppression of detailed anecdote.

Tjungurrayi in disguise   Nungala in disguise

journey sign   sit-down place

THEORIES OF PAPUNYA TULA ART

Technique and Symbology

N THEIR USE of lines and circles, and of primary color, the Papunya Tula paintings may be compared with paintings by children. However, whereas the child paints from intuition, the Western Desert painter is actually systematizing his intuitions in a most rigorous and self-conscious way. In his quest for a personal yet communally comprehensible form of expression, he brings his own modification and interpretation to an ancient and powerful set of symbols, and his own adaptation to traditional sand- and body-painting techniques.

The sand, body and tjurunga archetypes from which the Western Desert painting movement had sprung were much simpler, more circumscribed by social convention, than the paintings which had emerged at Papunya by July 1972, when I left the settlement. They often seemed solemn, almost liturgical, works in which a group of painters, working at the direction of (and for) the community, used black, red and white, and also yellow if available. The colors were earth colors and quite raw, and the painters would use honey ant tissue as a binding. The basic layout for the sand paintings was a Dreaming grid but it was free of the detailing and ornamentation of the later paintings. Whereas some painters now use colors from bottles, during my stay at Papunya I tried to develop the use of mixed earth colors in the paintings, so that the key colors were modified to more subtle red-browns, oranges, Naples-yellow and Indian red. Clifford Possum and Johnny Warrangkula had always competently mixed paints. But only after the first sale of Papunya paintings from a consignment which I brought to Alice Springs did a quantum leap take place in the painting, from an archetype to an expansive, complex and brilliant art form.

From earliest times Aboriginal designs have used a fixed range of colors: red, yellow, white and charcoal black, perhaps ash – the ochres most commonly

Artist Old Mick Tjakamarra (attributed)
Tribe Anmatjira Aranda
Born 1910
Story Possum Looking for Food in the Sandhills
Completed Early 1971
Size 15 × 36 cm (on cardboard)
Location North-north-west of the Macdonnell Ranges
Custodian Tjakamarra-Tjupurrula

The artist is using only the primal colours red, white and black ochre to tell a traditional story of a possum looking for food in the sandhills. There is great vitality in the stark alternation of black and white vertical lines for the area between the sandhills with white ochre for the sandhills themselves. The areas of red ochre give a sense of the earth surrounding and being included in everything. Note the simplicity of this painting compared with later ones by Old Mick.

found in the Australian desert. My advice to the Papunya painters was to retain the use of traditional ochres, with a bonding glue being introduced for permanence and adhesion. Some commercial paint and poster paint within the earth-color range were also used, but we generally avoided any clearly European colors (for example, blue or green).

The men instinctively showed quite brilliant judgement in their choice of colors. However, none of the painters (except perhaps Johnny Warrangkula) could be considered a colorist. It is probably more accurate to describe their use of color as tonal. Colors were generally used as shading, for a chiaroscuro effect, to articulate light and darkness in the paintings. Each color was a permutation of shadow and light and was understood more as it affected other colors than in its own right. Sometimes, color would be used to sustain and define the relationships between figures. The painters would superimpose a dissidence of colors one upon the other so as to conceptualize the landscape in tonal clusters within the frame. (This was spectacularly developed in the dotting techniques of Tim Leura and Mick Namerari.)

One of the more striking stylistics of Johnny Warrangkula Tjupurrula was his ability to set down apparently clashing colorations side by side. He seemed to work from an acceptance of the arbitrariness of color itself, implying that the form of the landscape emerges from this very arbitrariness.

The lack of uncertainty in the artists' execution of their work was highly significant. They painted into a predetermined background and without hesitation. The image put down seemed entirely conceived before the painting was begun, and there was no overpainting of forms. As a result, there was always an extraordinary immediacy about the work.

The base or floor of any Aboriginal design or painting is the preparation of the earth, or the ancestor being's involvement with the earth. The backgrounds of the desert paintings are often the action upon the sand of the honey ant, the Totemic Ancestor of the tribal groups at Papunya. In traditional sand paintings, this action was depicted by circles, loops and lines; in the Papunya paintings, cross-hatching and dotting are used.

Johnny Warrangkula was the first artist to use dotting as the background for his paintings. The other painters used hatching – or sometimes no design at all, leaving the background blank. Because of the brilliance of Johnny's work, however, quite a few of the other painters adopted his style and conventions.

Clifford Possum and Tim Leura, in particular, used Johnny Warrangkula's dotting technique with great effectiveness.

(As the painting movement developed, this technique was increasingly used to conceal meaning in the painting stories. Constant probing and questioning by white persons made the painters cautious about revealing secret-sacred issues in Aboriginal life. They tended to become conservative, denying the rich heritage of this secular Aboriginal art. Over some time, the simplicity and directness of the original technique has gradually given way to an ornamental style, a disguise, which has filled many recent paintings with a claustrophobic and oppressive sense of stillness. In these journeys there is no longer an impression of movement. A certain stolidity has taken over.)

The most commonly used symbols are relatively simple but can be used in more elaborate combinations. The graphic sign for a star had first interested me in the men's sand drawings. This seemed a wonderfully successful, valid sign for a perceived object.

Similarly, a fireplace is a stylized design using the elements and patterns of a fire. For a ceremony, corroboree men place fire-sticks by the fire. Later they hold the burning sticks aloft and flourish them in spectacular night rituals.

A simple Water Dreaming might show the classic U sign for a man, or human figure. The circle, or bull's-eye, is a waterhole, and the spiralling lines depict running water. The painter is telling the story of the power of the waterman to invoke rain.

Two old men are often shown sitting at a fire opposite each other eating sweet bush raisins which grow everywhere in sandhill areas. Viewed from above, the seated human figure forms a U shape. This is the motif accepted by the Central Australian Aborigines and used by the painters.

When the U shape is used in groups of four, it represents a Woman's Dreaming. Girls, with digging sticks, may beat the sand at fireplaces in mourning for a widow. There is a strict order at ceremonies as in all social arrangement. This is shown in the design layout of the painting, making the society's rule of order explicitly one of control.

A Sandhill Dreaming can show a journey across the landscape. The straight line with circles may represent travelling along the sandhills. The chain-like looping patterns can be dancing figures with boomerangs celebrating the journey. The painting may tell the elation of bountiful bush foraging after good

Artist Old Tutuma Tjapangati
Tribe Pintupi
Born c 1910 *Died* 1986
Story Fireplaces, Spears and Stars at Night
Completed Pre-1971
Size Approximately 30 × 45 cm
Location West of Papunya
Custodian Tjapangati-Tjapananga

It was the motif of a star that first interested me in the men's sand paintings.

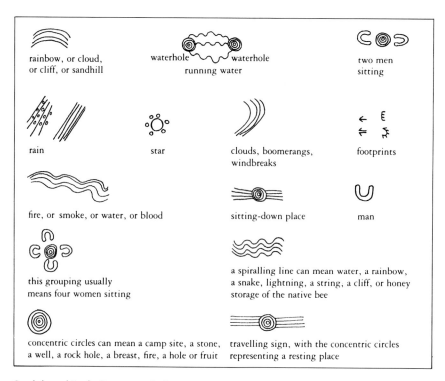

Symbols used in the Papunya paintings

rain. The people are content, and the journey continues as a rapture and a celebration.

In corroboree stories, the big claypans are shown by concentric circles. Weaving lines are the paths of the corroboree men as they move about the claypan, preparing for the ceremonies. The small concentric circles may represent many men seated around the corroboree stick, which can be a special pole erected at the corroboree place.

Balance, rhythm, symmetry, tension and design consciousness are all elements resulting from the three-dimensionality of tjurunga patterning, coolamon and shield decoration, spears and so on. The clever usage of these elements by the Papunya artists is a fair measure of their adaptability, mental organization and intelligence and of the fundamentally aesthetic quality of their living culture.

Hapticity

Post-renaissance European culture generally emphasizes visual phenomena in art, but the Aboriginal temperament has always been haptic: it has a predilec-

PHOTOGRAPH: ALLAN SCOTT

Kaapa Tjampitjinpa telling a painting story by touching, 1972.

tion for the sensitivity of touch, for the physical, the tactile. We know from archives that traditional designs in rock carvings, weapons decoration and tjurunga patterning were created by chipping into a stone or wooden object, and sand mosaics and body decoration were created by finger painting with ochre colors and feathers. Accordingly, the designs were read by touch and did not necessarily involve visual perception.

Whereas painting is widely assumed to be an unquestionably visual art, the Aborigine telling a tjurunga Dreaming will feel the incised scoring in the stone or wood, and move his hand along the lines and so across the object. He also adopts this attitude when painting and when explaining the work – by hand signs, pointing, and freely touching the board. The man understands and reveals his work by touching it, not necessarily by looking at it. The men at Papunya, I noticed, seemed to have great difficulty copying – in visual terms – a successful earlier work. This is because the origin and meaning of the painting do not depend on eyesight and visual sensation; they are subjective, and the artist himself has to tell his story and reveal the psychological reality of his spiritual relationship to his Dreaming. This is a higher realism, a transcendental interaction of man, his spirit and his world. The concept of a 'picture', and the idea of the 'pictorial', where a visual object is related to a spatial area, are therefore unhelpful in describing Western Desert painting.

A long European insistence on visual sensibility, and its integral dominance of school education, have brought about a decline in Aboriginal haptic sensibility. Aboriginal children today have a perplexing compulsion to handle and touch things, to feel walls, motor cars, friendly visitors. And yet, as though they were blind, little provision is made for them to function within these intuitions, and they are deemed slow to learn.

Because of this influence, each Papunya artist can be considered in terms of his contact with European culture. The bush Pintupi are universally haptic, with flat, one-dimensional patterns; they are least affected by European culture. The Loritja and Wailpri seem to be an intermediate group at Papunya, in that they use flat patterns with suggestions of perspective and symmetrical order in the balance of the design. The Anmatjira Aranda regularly suggest three-dimensional qualities, are willing to use realistic illustration, and can even be described as primarily visual painters. They have experienced the strongest European influence. However, these artists still use traditional motifs and forms modified by naturalism, realism and three-dimensional spatiality.

The Fourth Dimension

The European visual tradition and its conventional understanding of perspective were called into question in the early twentieth century by Cubist painters such as Marcel Duchamp and Suprematist painters such as Kasimir Malevich. Like the Aboriginal artists before them, they esteemed the tactile quality of pictorial space along with the visual, and sought to perceive and depict a fourth dimension in their art. However, whereas with Marcel Duchamp it was the rotation of the painting which could induce the fourth-dimensional idea, with Aboriginal art it is walking around the painting or, in its original sand form, walking through the painting. This capacity to both encircle the painting and enter into it is at the heart of the dimensionality of Western Desert art. The painters seem to feel most at ease with their story when it is seen from all directions at once and seen 'through'.

'Family Bush Tucker Dreaming' by Mick Namerari (See page 88) shows the human proponents of the story in such a way that the viewer sees through their bodies and also through the bush shelters in which each person is sleeping. The fireplace is seen from above, as are the sleeping humans. The painting simultaneously apprehends the witchetty grub and the humans as equal aspects of the story/landscape. The witchetty grub is depicted on the same scale as the three humans shown alongside it. Just as form follows function so is the story essentially that of the equivalence between the human figures and what they are eating (or have eaten).

A long tradition of 'painting' on the ground has provided the Aborigines with an almost instinctive bird's-eye perspective of all images – including photographs, which they look at upside-down or any way at all. Rather than distorting appearance within the painting (as did the Cubists) the Papunya artists provide a sense of the arbitrariness and hence absolute relativity of the painting's edge. This relativity, which denies any certainty other than the apparently unlimited points of view from which the painting can be observed, is the fourth dimensional cloak, or frame, of the perceptual third dimension, stemming directly from the sand-mosaic and body-painting mediums.

The Western Desert painters do not oppose themselves to the world, but actually enter into the world. There is no perspectival tradition to distance them from what they see. They bring the horizon into the landscape as clouds, rain, hail, atmospheric disturbance. Since infinity is understood as the depicted land itself, there is no visual idea of infinity. The cosmological elements are enumerated without the emotional need to stand outside the landscape. The closeness to what is seen is arguably the relationship people had to the land in much earlier times; it is perhaps prehistoric, neolithic. Though it is not suggested that we should try to inhabit a neolithic culture, the entry into landscape, using the desert symbology, may yet in some degree allow us visually to comprehend a landscape which seems to deny any already understood idea of form.

The extensive graphic vocabulary of the Western Desert painters is a stylized enactment of the various elements of desert life and therefore can accurately be seen as hieroglyphic. The Western Desert hieroglyphs may be categorized as entirely abstract or as semi-abstract, although this difference depends on a twentieth-century European understanding of abstraction. The painters appear to understand space as an emotional idea, or form, or hieroglyph, and their capacity to feel the hieroglyph seems often to exclude any need to visualize what is represented. The painters have given emotional coherence to the idea of space

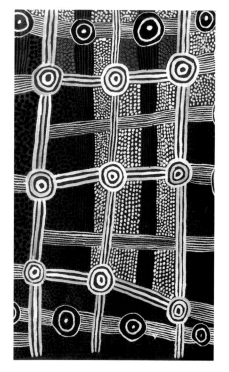

Striking examples of the strength of the hieroglyph in Papunya Tula art, painted in 1971 or 1972 (by unknown Pintupi artists).

by assuming something that has been lost to other cultures for millennia: that one *sees* in relation to an existing social organization.

The desert hieroglyphs appear to deny the very capacity of the landscape to be formed by the eye. And this is of course their strength, for they talk to the acceptance of formlessness, to the understanding that form itself is arbitrary. The paintings, as transcriptions of sand paintings, are representations and embodiments of matter. By reducing, or averaging, form, the hieroglyphs allow a visual and conceptual understanding of our exterior world. In the original sand paintings the painters could, in an instant and at will, change a hieroglyph, making it neither exclusive nor permanent. The same story could be rearranged into endless variants of hieroglyph clusters. There is no sense of words being read simultaneously with an image, for the word and the image are the same. It is as though the entire landscape were made up of a lexicon in which visual 'words', in their apparently inexhaustible interrelationships, dynamically create and recreate the landscape apprehended by the painters.

This interaction, this creative principle, can be seen as a form of grammar, in which the hieroglyph itself is a noun; the use of colors, intensifications, stresses and clarifications is the adjective or adverb; and the continual remaking and reconstitution of their relativity in space, the dynamic re-forming, is the verb.

As simultaneity is pre-eminently a symbolic way of reducing all understanding to space, the hieroglyph becomes idiomatic, contingent, provisional, qualified by its dynamic relationship with other hieroglyphs: Each hieroglyph can mean different things according to its disposition within the frame and its relationship to other hieroglyphs, directing, refracting and accommodating its relationship with other hieroglyphs.

Clifford Possum's 'Man's Love Story' (See page 115) is a fine example of simultaneity and four-dimensionality. Time and space are imposed one upon the other, the cloud upon the earth where the old man is seen (by his footsteps) approaching the fireplace at which he is singing. He is depicted coming towards the fireplace as well as seeing himself approach, making a string to catch a woman. It is as though one were looking down at the ground beneath one's feet at this painting and imagining the designed and patterned earth as an immense centrifuge. The same place perceived at different moments (as in Clifford's 'Man's Love Story') and the same moment perceived at different places (as in Mick Namerari's 'Witchetty Grub Family Dreaming') show the energy which the Western Desert painters idealize in the landscape.

The desert hieroglyphs and their simultaneity are an archetypal expression of human consciousness, the coming together of image and word in unsurpassed harmony. The return of the gods, perhaps.

The Re-perception of the Continent

Tim Leura once said to me that he thought that the paintings on board or canvas were only toys. He also said that the idea of a permanent artefact was the white man's.

The corroboree was only an ephemeral event and after the ceremony the sand mosaics were allowed to blow away. The idea, however, and the form within which the particular Dreaming was comprehended, were eternal. The eternal idea could be made into the visual representation of what the corroboree and its singing and dancing affirmed. The great idea was invisible, like the Spirit Ancestors of the painting men. Landscape could be form to these men: there was no part of the earth within their experience of it that did not have a meaning.

After 1971, the Western Desert painters, using European materials, were defining themselves within certain perceptions of the continent that were many thousands of years old. Their commitment of sand painting, or tjurunga or body painting, to board or canvas gave each story a new durability: once put down, it could not be erased. Because of the demands of the new form the use of space within the form became quite different from that space in the traditional telling. In the original sand mosaics and body designs, space continually expanded in relation to the story being narrated. Now, the frame was to become a metaphor for the greater space beyond the perimeter. It was the painter's instinctive defiance of any arbitrary physical limitation to what was told which gave the painting such power and emotional resonance.

The simultaneity of form and idea in the landscape implies that all the happenings represented take place at once in the stated area and that the landscape is the form. This landscape is a creation by eternal forces beyond time. The land surface was the manifestation of the Totemic Ancestors and it had no temporality and was therefore beyond any understanding of time such as we have. Simultaneity, in this sense, is an eternal present. It is a means of seeing a painting from any position, floating as it were – originally upon the sands, and now in eternity.

The concept of simultaneity and the use of the frame as a metaphor had a powerful resonance in Europe in the early twentieth century, particularly in the work of Robert Delaunay. Wassily Kandinsky and Paul Klee and many other painters adopted positions consistent with both the relativism of all perception and the idea that temporality is within ourselves.

In the Western Desert paintings, the images do not provide a mere graphic equivalent of spoken words, thereby attaching themselves to the temporality implicit in the ordinary syntax of a sentence. Quite to the contrary, and importantly: time has become space. There is no conventional sequentiality in the 'stories', but rather the accretion of space or 'place'. Since the space or 'place' is only the retelling of a story already known to the painter, the so-called 'story' is an eternal idea in the culture of the painter. The elements or images of the story therefore have no reading direction as we understand it.

In the European painting tradition the horizon may be a metaphor for a division between earth and sky, or for the boundedness of the earth. Perspective articulates humans in their environment and visually represents the need humans have felt, most famously since the Renaissance, to separate themselves from the earth while seeming to enter into it.

Since the efflorescence and decline of the Streeton-Roberts school of impressionism there has been a continual searching among Australian painters for an emotionally valid approach to the country's landscape. The paintings of John Olsen and Fred Williams show where the search has led. These two artists have tended to use — sometimes as quotations, sometimes as borrowed conventions — the Western Desert iconography of hieroglyph and form. But one senses continually the tenuousness of their gaze. In the absence of the genre story of the Heidelberg tradition, there is strain in these artists' way of looking at the landscape.

By contrast, Old Mick Tjakamarra's 'Children's Water Dreaming with Possum Story' (See page 69) shows clouds on the ground with the rocks and creeks. The depiction of sky is resolved spatially and without the need for the internal horizon so often seen in Fred Williams's paintings.

Fred Williams and John Olsen look at their country from a very great distance and their forms are complicated, circumstantial and tentative. Williams is brilliant but seems unable to sustain, conceptually, the absence of horizon. There is always a horizon in Williams. The Papunya painters have no need for internal or external horizons; their horizons lie within the landscape.

The Western Desert paintings are never conceived of as a physical limitation upon the ability to see. Furthermore the perspective picture plane or constraints such as those of Alberti's celebrated 'window' do not seem to be among the desert painters' conventions. This absence of horizon is a legacy of the sand paintings: there was no natural perspective and no induced perspective other than that which the topography allowed. This desert topography, and to some extent the constraints of the framing introduced by me in 1971 and 1972, are central in the extraordinary development of the painting movement, for the paintings during this period testified to an enormous quantum or conceptual leap.

Since the origins of the movement lay in the strict adherence by tribal painters to designs and collaborations accepted by the community as an expression of its culture, the change to expanded and extraordinarily detailed paintings of stories that could not have been represented either in the sand or upon the tjurungas, stones, caves or human bodies acquires prime importance in any understanding of the movement.

The pre-painting that was carried out upon the sand was defined only by the tribal connotations of its story. The story could go in any direction, for it was the story and its telling, and not conventions such as the European horizon, which determined the disposition of what was shown. The Western Desert paintings are not primarily visual, but rather a mutation of haptic and visual ideograms and hieroglyphs enacting an idea which is pre-ordained by the landscape shown.

Kaapa Tjampitjinpa tended to remain a traditional iconographer, but Tim Leura, Clifford Possum and Johnny Warrangkula in particular all developed quite startling variants and modifications of their tribal contexts. Their designs became highly linear, and they used lines and aspects of lines to define shapes simply and effectively and to create a shallow depth of field. By combining existing hieroglyphs with a daring use of color and calligraphic intensities and an imaginative use of human and animal shapes, they showed the way towards a new art form.

To the Aboriginal people the great deserts are like a heaven of constellated stars which are named in order to be seen. The 'words' used to describe this 'sky' of sand, mountains and trees are conceived visually by the people, and this is essentially what a hieroglyph is. The malleability of the sand is the strength of the hieroglyphs and accounts for the suppleness, variety and fecundity of the formings (as the hieroglyphs may also be called), since their irreducibility is in essence a becoming.

The hieroglyph is a gestural word, a thing in itself, and the painters' ideographic vocabulary is a systematic use of the environment to form meaning clusters, or 'words'. The paintings are calligraphic, austerely linear visualizations. The originality of the late painting of May to July 1972 seemed to me to arise in part because this vocabulary was retained, and the sand did talk, and also in part because the gestural, hieroglyphic articulations were expanded by abstract yet highly Aboriginal figurations of animals, birds and men. These extensions of the hieroglyph were credible, brilliant and right. A way into the continent not understood by us before had emerged, as in some fable, from the very sand on which we stood.

After 1979, a subtle change came about in the paintings at Papunya and its flourishing out-stations. At about this time, the painters seem to have omitted the hieroglyphs which spoke to what was being done, and often simply covered an area with an intense patterning, brightly colored and symmetrically right.

Incredibly, the desert painters began to circumscribe their stories and deny the incisiveness and explicitness of their motifs, marginalizing the symbolism and idealisation of color and line. The result was sometimes bland, symmetrical designs and dim, recessive and floridly trivial work. The desert hieroglyph script, arguably the only original art form to have emerged from the Australian continent, was endangered.

I believe it is in the furthest reaches of the human imagination that our country lies, and there we must seek it out, like poets of a coming age. The Western Desert painters, almost by an incredible act of fate, have given Australians a way into the continent. The history of the continent has thus been changed forever.

LOOKING BACK

OST STARTLING when you flew over the settlement after the beginning of the painting movement was the configuration now identifiable beneath as Papunya: a huge red-brown bull's-eye with lines extending in all directions from the centre and across the plain. You had a sense of a massing of shapes within the central force of what was below. The central bull's-eye could have been the representation of a fire, or a waterhole, or a hill, or a camp, or a woman, or all of them at once, and the lines outward were the men's travelling directions from the centre of what you saw. Papunya itself was a Dreaming design or hieroglyph, proclaimed as such by its peoples after the beginning of the movement. This was in part what the Dreaming meant.

Papunya in 1971 saw a vast upsurge of the human spirit, when a gifted people, oppressed by years of hatred, stood up once more. The painting movement allowed them to relive their magnificent past and achieve self-respect. If some painters broke tribal laws by revealing secrets and sacrednesses, this was, I feel now, only the action of a desperate people trying to express feelings which had been buried by their authoritarian and quite uncomprehending white controllers. Their miraculous and exultant art was a marvellous cause after righteousness itself. It was like the camp fires on the Papunya glade: a kind of incandescence which, in 1971–72, became a great artistic and spiritual conflagration among the desert tribes.

The Aborigines have a fierce longing for, and identification with, their beloved land. That love, of course, was what the painting movement was always about. Yet it is no ordinary love, but something so passionate and all-involving that the most appalling genocide and degradation could not stop its course.

One thing is certain: through the art of the Western Desert, European occupation of Australia has been brought, quite extraordinarily, within a parenthesis.

EPILOGUE

AFTER I LEFT Papunya in 1972 Tim Leura's great 'Yam Spirit Dreaming', which I had bought from him with my leather coat, was lost. I was told how, after I left the settlement, the painters' quarters were ransacked and every painting there was carried away. Apparently with the consent of the authorities, all paintings that could be found were loaded onto a government vehicle and taken out of Papunya.

I learned later that many paintings were sold by the government employees without the consent of the painters. The problem so often at Papunya and in the Western Desert was that the Aboriginal people had to take what they were given. The Europeans had little or no sense of accountability. Alice Springs seemed often to corrupt whatever presumptions to honesty that the whites had. The disease-ridden, dispossessed and politically and financially powerless blacks were treated as animals hardly fit to beg. It was all like that: the sneer, the patronizing word or gesture, the refusal to accept that a black man should be paid in full, or as a full man, for what he did.

I returned to Papunya about a year later to begin some research for my book. The school murals had been suppressed, painted over by the authorities, and I felt that there had been an awful drift by the painters away from their true selves. Yet it is strange how, as in some stories, something of love and worth can be saved if the decent thought is there. I recall going about the camp, calling on some white friends. 'We've got something for you, Geoff,' one of them said. To my astonishment they brought out Tim Leura's 'Yam Spirit Dreaming' – one of the most beautiful of all Papunya paintings, which had been lost. It was quite intact, quite undisturbed, in its majestic way.

Then I was told of how, when the paintings had been taken away, it had been hidden behind a cupboard in a manual arts room for an entire year; how

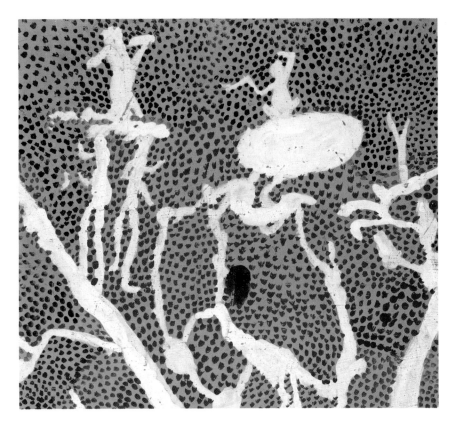

Detail of Tim Leura Tjapaltjarri's 'Yam Spirit Dreaming' (See page 120).

everything else had been taken from the settlement after I left, yet for some reason this painting had remained safely hidden for so long. It was almost, I thought, like a beloved child restored joyfully to its doting father when he thought it murdered and vanished.

The quality of the strong is measured by their treatment of the weak. There is some kind of damnation upon a society which allows men and women to be found in the condition of the desert Aborigines after so much has been done for them in selflessness and love.

The Western Desert paintings raise questions concerning the corruption and exploitation of Aboriginal people. Daisy Bates could not bring herself to leave them . . . 'There is no one else to do my work because no one else is willing to live as I lived,' she wrote.

If these people fail as individuals, then, because of that faithfulness to each other within their tribal duty, they fail together. You will always wonder what will happen to them.

BIBLIOGRAPHY

Apollonio, Umbro, 1973, *Futurist Manifestos (Documents of 20th Century Art)*, The Viking Press

Arnheim, Rudolf, 1969, *Visual Thinking*, University of California Press

Boaz, Franz, 1955, *Primitive Art*, Dover Publications Inc.

Brody, Anne Marie, 1986, *The Face of the Centre: Papunya Tula Paintings 1971–1984*, National Gallery of Victoria

Goldwater, Robert, 1986, *Primitivism in Modern Art*, The Belknap Press of Harvard University Press

Gombrich, E H, 1983, *Art and Illusion*, Phaidon Press

Gombrich, E H, Hockberg, Julian, and Black, Max, 1980, *Art, Perception and Reality*, John Hopkins University Press

Henderson, Linda Dalrymple, 1983, *The Fourth Dimension in Modern Art*, Princeton University Press

Kandinsky, Wassily, and Marc, Franz (eds), 1974, *The Blaue Reiter Almanac (Documents of 20th Century Art)*, The Viking Press

Magaw, Vincent (ed), 1984, *Dot and Circle*, Royal Melbourne Institute of Technology

Munn, Nancy, 1974, *Wailbri Iconography*, University of Chicago Press

Ouspensky, P D, 1982, *Tertium Organum*, Routledge & Kegan Paul

Panofsky, Erwin, 1968, *Idea, a Concept in Art Theory*, Harper & Row

Perloff, Marjorie, 1986, *The Futurist Movement*, University of Chicago Press

Ryan, Judith, 1989, *Mythscapes: Aboriginal Art of the Western Desert*, National Gallery of Victoria

Sperber, Dan, 1979, *Rethinking Symbolism*, University of Cambridge Press

Ucko, Peter J, 1978, *Form in Indigenous Art*, Australian Institute of Aboriginal Studies